The Budget Meal Planner

Save Money and Time While Eating Better

Julie Anne Summer

Mt Trogon Creative

Book cover by Majid Khan

First edition 2025

Contents

Introduction   2

1. Budget Meal Planning Fundamentals   4
   Building Your Money-Saving Kitchen Foundation

2. Smart Shopping Strategies   23
   Maximizing Value at Every Store Type

3. The Art of Batch Cooking   41
   Small-Scale Success for Solo Cooks

4. Quick Prep, Big Savings   59
   Time-Efficient Meal Solutions

5. Frugal Family Favorites   82
   Scaling Recipes for Any Household

6. Love Your Leftovers   100
   Creative Solutions for Zero Waste

7. Special Diets, Savvy Budget   117
   Accommodating Restrictions Without Breaking the Bank

8. Budget-Friendly Entertainment   138
   Hosting Without the High Costs

Conclusion   157

Also By   161
Julie Anne Summers

References / Bibliography   164

Dedication

To all the culinary adventurers who dare to create magic in the kitchen, and those who've learned that a little planning can save a lot of dough (and maybe a few tears).

Introduction

Standing in my kitchen one Wednesday evening, surrounded by takeout containers and a dwindling bank balance, I realized something had to change. Like many busy professionals, I had fallen into the convenient but costly habit of relying on delivery services and pre-made meals. That moment became my catalyst for transformation – not just of my eating habits, but of my entire relationship with food and finances.

The journey wasn't always smooth. I remember my first attempt at meal planning ended with an overflowing freezer, mismatched containers, and the humbling realization that I had much to learn about kitchen efficiency. But with each small success – from mastering the art of repurposing leftovers to discovering the joy of batch cooking in my tiny apartment kitchen – I found myself growing more confident and capable.

Over the past decade, I've transformed my kitchen from a takeout hub to a thriving meal prep sanctuary. Through recession-era budgeting and modern-day inflation, I've learned that eating well doesn't require deep pockets – it requires strategy, creativity, and a willingness to learn. Whether you're cooking for one or feeding a family, dealing with dietary restrictions, or simply trying to stretch your grocery budget further, this book is your roadmap to affordable, delicious, and nutritious meals.

In these pages, you'll find more than just recipes and meal plans. You'll discover practical strategies for navigating different types of grocery stores, techniques for reducing food waste, and methods for adapting recipes to various dietary needs. I'll share my hard-earned insights on everything from organizing a small kitchen for maximum efficiency to hosting budget-friendly gatherings that don't feel cheap.

This isn't about extreme couponing or surviving on rice and beans. It's about smart, sustainable approaches to food that respect both your budget and your taste buds. We'll explore how to build a flexible meal planning system that adapts to changing food prices and your schedule. You'll learn to transform simple ingredients into satisfying meals and discover how proper storage and creative leftovers can stretch your food budget further than you ever imagined.

The budgeting lessons I learned during the 2008 recession have only become more relevant in today's economic climate. Whether you're a college student learning to cook, a busy professional trying to cut costs, or someone who simply wants to make their grocery budget work harder, you'll find practical, actionable advice that meets you where you are.

Remember, successful budget meal planning isn't about deprivation – it's about empowerment. It's about taking control of your food budget while creating meals that nourish both body and soul. Together, we'll explore how to make your kitchen work harder for you, saving both time and money while eating better than ever before.

Let's begin this journey of turning financial constraints into culinary creativity, one meal at a time.

Enjoy!

Julie x

Chapter One

Budget Meal Planning Fundamentals

Building Your Money-Saving Kitchen Foundation

As we begin this journey, remember that creating an efficient, budget-friendly kitchen isn't about having the latest gadgets or the most expensive organizational systems. It's about understanding the basic principles of kitchen management and applying them in ways that work for your situation. Whether you're working with a tiny apartment kitchen or a spacious cooking area, the fundamentals we'll cover will help you build a strong foundation for successful budget meal planning.

In this chapter, we'll break down these essential components into manageable steps, helping you assess your current kitchen setup and transform it into an efficient workspace that supports your budget-friendly cooking goals. From organizing your space to selecting the right tools and establishing smart shopping habits, you'll learn how small, strategic changes can lead to significant savings over time.

These foundational elements aren't just about saving money—they're about creating a sustainable system that makes cooking at home enjoyable and economical. With proper planning and organization, maintaining a budget-friendly kitchen will become second nature, leaving you more time and energy to focus on creating delicious, nutritious meals that don't break the bank.

Essential Kitchen Tools and Equipment: What You Really Need

When I started my budget cooking journey, I believed I needed every gadget advertised on late-night cooking shows to create delicious meals. My kitchen drawers were bursting with rarely used specialty items, while my bank account was significantly lighter. It wasn't until I accidentally left most of my kitchen tools in storage during a move that I discovered that you need far fewer tools than you might think to cook efficiently and economically.

Let's start with the absolute essentials - the workhorses of a budget-friendly kitchen that earn their keep through daily use.

Absolute Essentials
- Chef's knife (8-inch) and paring knife

- Large cutting board (wood or plastic)

- Large stainless steel mixing bowl

- Measuring cups and spoons

- Large stockpot (6-8 quart)

- 12-inch skillet with lid

- 3-quart saucepan with lid

- Sheet pan

- Colander

- Basic utensils (wooden spoon, spatula, tongs)

The beauty of this essential list is that each item serves multiple purposes, eliminating the need for single-use gadgets that often collect dust. For instance, that large mixing bowl isn't just for combining ingredients

- it can serve as a salad bowl, a vessel for marinating proteins, or even a makeshift proving bowl for bread dough. The stockpot works for everything from soups and stews to cooking pasta or steaming vegetables.

I learned this lesson hard during my first year of budget cooking. I had spent nearly $200 on specialty items like an avocado slicer, a mushroom brush, and various other single-purpose tools, only to find myself consistently reaching for the same essential items. That money could have been better spent on a high-quality chef's knife - an investment that would have made food preparation faster, safer, and more enjoyable.

Speaking of knives, this is one area where it's worth investing a bit more. A chef's knife can last for years with proper care, making food preparation significantly more manageable and safer. Look for sales at kitchen or restaurant supply stores offering reasonably priced professional-grade equipment. Remember, you're better off with one good knife than a drawer full of mediocre ones.

As your cooking skills and budget grow, you might consider expanding:

Secondary Tools

- Food storage containers (various sizes)

- Box grater

- Instant-read thermometer

- Immersion blender

- Kitchen scale

- Baking dish (9x13 inch)

These additional items can make meal prep more efficient and open up new recipe possibilities, but they're not essential for starting.

Considering any new kitchen purchase, ask yourself:
- Will this tool serve multiple purposes?

- How often will I realistically use it?

- Could I accomplish the same task with tools I already own?

I've found that focusing on versatile, durable equipment rather than trendy gadgets not only saves money initially but also reduces clutter and maintenance costs over time. For example, while an electric rice cooker might seem convenient, a simple saucepan with a tight-fitting lid can cook perfect rice while being available for countless other cooking tasks.

Remember that building your kitchen arsenal doesn't have to happen simultaneously. Start with the essentials and add pieces gradually as you identify genuine needs in your cooking routine. Many of my most-used tools came from thrift stores and restaurant supply stores or were handed down from family members. The key is focusing on quality and versatility rather than quantity and novelty.

When storing your tools, keep frequently used items within easy reach of your primary work area. This simple organization strategy saves time and makes cooking more enjoyable. I arrange my tools based on their frequency of use—everyday items stay at the counter level, while special-occasion tools live in higher cabinets or deeper drawers.

Building a Budget-Friendly Pantry: Strategic Staples and Storage

The heart of any budget-friendly kitchen lies in a well-stocked, strategically organized pantry. I figured this out the hard way during my first month of budget cooking when I made multiple mid-week grocery runs for essential ingredients, each trip resulting in unnecessary impulse purchases. These extra trips cost me not only money but also valuable time. That's when I realized that building an intelligent pantry system wasn't just about storing food but creating a foundation for efficient, economical meal planning.

Essential Pantry Staples
- **Grains:** rice, pasta, oats, quinoa

- **Legumes**: dried or canned beans, lentils, split peas

- **Canned goods:** tomatoes, tuna, vegetables

- **Cooking oils**: olive oil, vegetable oil

- **Vinegars:** white, apple cider, rice

- **Basic spices**: black pepper, cumin, paprika, oregano

- **Baking essentials**: flour, sugar, baking powder, baking soda

---

Proper storage is key to effectively maintaining these staples. I gained insight from a difficult lesson for what I refer to as my 'Great Flour Fiasco'—discovering weevils in an improperly stored bag of flour taught me the importance of airtight containers and proper rotation systems. Now, I use clear, airtight containers for all dry goods, which allows me to easily monitor inventory levels and protect against pests.

When it comes to building your pantry, start small and expand gradually. Focus first on ingredients that serve multiple purposes and align with your cooking style. For instance, don't invest heavily in baking supplies if you rarely bake. Instead, concentrate on the staples you'll use most frequently in cooking.

One of the most effective strategies I utilize is a 'three-tier' pantry organization. The first tier contains everyday items that need to be easily accessible. The second tier holds backup supplies and less frequently used items. The third tier is for bulk items and seasonal ingredients. This system helps prevent food waste by ensuring nothing gets lost in the back of the pantry.

Pricing and purchasing strategy play crucial roles in building a budget-friendly pantry. I maintain a price book to track the lowest prices I've found for staple items across different stores. This helps me recognize genuine deals and decide when to stock up. For example, my local ethnic grocery store offers rice at nearly half the price of major supermarkets, while my neighborhood discount store has the best prices on canned goods.

Storage solutions don't need to be expensive. While matching glass containers look beautiful, clean recycled jars also work. The key is ensuring containers are airtight and properly labelled with contents and purchase dates. I use a simple rotation system—new items go to the back, older items stay in front—to prevent food waste.

Another crucial aspect of pantry management is understanding shelf life and storage conditions. Different ingredients require different environments to maintain their quality. For instance, whole grain flour should be stored in the refrigerator to prevent rancidity, while white flour can be kept at room temperature. Spices should be stored away from heat and direct sunlight to maintain potency.

One of my most successful pantry strategies has been creating a collection of shelf-stable ingredients that can form the base of several different meals. For example, a simple kit might include pasta, canned tomatoes, and basic Italian seasonings - add different fresh ingredients, and you can create numerous variations of quick, affordable meals.

Remember that a well-stocked pantry is an investment that pays dividends in both time and money saved. You're less likely to resort to expensive takeout or last-minute grocery runs when you have the right ingredients. Start small, build gradually, and focus on ingredients that align with your cooking style and dietary needs. With proper organization and storage, your pantry can become the cornerstone of your budget-friendly kitchen.

Smart Shopping Fundamentals: Store Selection and Shopping Strategies

My first lesson in smart shopping came from an embarrassing moment at my local grocery store. Standing in the cereal aisle, comparing prices between two boxes, I realized I was looking at the total price rather than the unit price—a mistake that had cost me money for months. This simple revelation changed my entire approach to grocery shopping and became the foundation of my strategic shopping method.

Understanding different store types and their pricing strategies is crucial for maximizing your grocery budget. Each type of store offers distinct advantages.

Different store type advantages

- **Discount grocery stores**: Lower overall prices, excellent for shelf-stable basics

- **Traditional supermarkets**: Better produce selection, frequent sales on name brands

- **Warehouse clubs**: Bulk pricing advantages for non-perishables and freezer items

- **Ethnic markets**: Often better prices on spices, produce, and international ingredients

- **Farmers markets**: Seasonal produce, often with end-of-day discounts

---

The key to successful budget shopping isn't finding the cheapest store—it's about knowing which items to buy where. I have mapped out the best prices for my commonly purchased items across different stores in my area. This revealed that while my local discount store had the best prices on canned goods and dairy, the ethnic market offered significantly better deals on rice, spices, and certain produce items.

One of the most valuable skills I've developed is understanding store layouts and shopping patterns. Most supermarkets follow similar design principles, placing essential items like dairy and bread at the back of the store to encourage customers to walk past tempting displays. I now organize my shopping lists by store section, which not only saves time but also helps me resist impulse purchases by keeping me focused on my planned items.

Timing can significantly impact your grocery budget. I discovered that shopping early in the morning often gives access to the best produce selection and marked-down items from the previous day. Many stores also offer better deals mid-week when there's less shopping traffic. Learning your stores' markdown schedules for perishable items like meat and bread can also lead to substantial savings.

Unit pricing became my secret weapon for smart shopping. Instead of looking at package prices, I compared the cost per ounce or pound. This practice revealed that the 'family size' package isn't always the better deal, and sometimes store brands are more expensive per unit than name brands on sale. I keep a small notebook with standard unit prices, which helps me quickly identify genuine bargains.

Loyalty programs and digital coupons have become increasingly important tools for strategic shopping. However, I learned to approach these tools with caution. The key is using them for items you plan to buy rather than letting them drive your purchases. I maintain a simple rule: if it wasn't on my list and I don't need it within the next two weeks, it's not a deal - it's an unnecessary expense.

Another of my most effective shopping strategies is always shopping with a list. I leave about 20% of my budget flexible to take advantage of unexpected sales on staple items. This approach allows me to stock up on frequently used items at their lowest price while maintaining overall budget control.

Store brands deserve special attention in any smart shopping strategy. Through careful testing, I've found that store brands offer identical quality at significant savings for many essential items - flour, sugar, and canned vegetables. However, there are certain items where name brands make a difference in quality. The key is testing selectively and noting which store brands work for your needs.

Remember that smart shopping isn't just about finding the lowest prices - it's about maximizing the value of every dollar spent. This means considering factors like food quality, storage life, and how likely you are to use the item before it spoils. A great deal on bulk perishables isn't a deal if half ends up in the compost bin.

Most importantly, successful budget shopping requires patience and consistency. It takes time to learn price patterns, discover the best sources for different items, and develop efficient shopping routines. Start by focusing on the items you buy most frequently, tracking their prices across various stores, and gradually building your knowledge of where to find the best values for your needs.

⊱⋅ ⋅⊰

Meal Planning Basics: Creating Your First Weekly Plan

My journey into meal planning began with a 'Week of Random Dinners' - seven days of staring into my refrigerator at 6 PM, hoping inspiration would strike. Not only did this approach waste time and energy, but it also led to numerous takeout orders and unused ingredients wilting in my produce drawer. I realized that successful budget cooking starts with a solid meal plan.

Steps to Effective Meal Planning

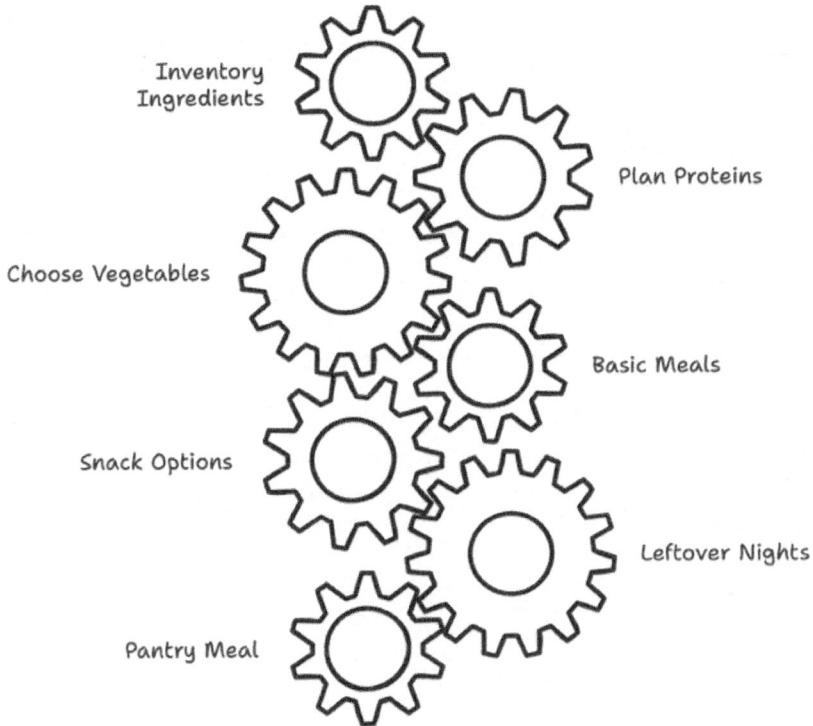

Inventory
Ingredients

Plan Proteins

Choose Vegetables

Basic Meals

Snack Options

Leftover Nights

Pantry Meal

Creating your first weekly meal plan might seem daunting, but I've developed a simple system that breaks it down into manageable steps. Start by taking inventory of what you already have - this prevents duplicate purchases and ensures you use ingredients before they spoil. I keep a magnetic notepad on my refrigerator where I list items that need to be used soon, making them the starting point for my weekly plan.

> **Essential components of a successful meal plan:**
> - **Primary protein sources** for each dinner
>
> - **Versatile vegetables** that can be used in multiple dishes
>
> - **Breakfast and lunch basics**
>
> - **Snack options**
>
> - **Planned leftover** nights
>
> - One flexible '**pantry meal**' using shelf-stable ingredients

The key to sustainable meal planning is starting small. Begin with planning just dinners for the week, then gradually expand to include other meals as you become more comfortable with the process. I learned this lesson after an overly ambitious attempt to plan three meals a day plus snacks, which left me feeling overwhelmed and ready to give up entirely.

When selecting recipes for your meal plan, consider a crossover ingredient strategy. This involves choosing dishes that share common ingredients to minimize waste and maximize your grocery budget. For example, if you're buying fresh herbs for one recipe, plan another meal to use the remainder before they spoil. This approach saves money and helps maintain variety in your meals while keeping your shopping list manageable.

One of my most effective planning tools is a '3-3-1' formula: three new recipes from your current ingredients, three favorites that you know by heart, and one 'clean out the fridge' meal. This balance helps prevent meal fatigue while keeping your budget and time commitment realistic. It also builds flexibility for busy days or unexpected changes in your schedule.

Weather and seasonality should influence your meal planning. I learned this lesson during a summer heat wave when I had planned several oven-heavy meals. Now, I check the weather forecast before finalizing my weekly plan, choosing slow-cooker meals for hot days and saving more involved cooking projects for cooler weather. This approach makes cooking more enjoyable and helps take advantage of seasonal ingredients when they're most affordable.

Creating a shopping list is an integral part of meal planning. I organize mine by store section (produce, dairy, pantry, etc.) and include specific quantities needed for each recipe. This organization prevents overbuying and helps stick to budget constraints. I also maintain a 'price awareness' column on my list where I note the expected cost of items based on previous shopping trips, which helps identify when prices have increased significantly and adjustments might be needed.

Remember to build flexibility into your plan. I always include one or two 'pantry meals'—simple dishes made entirely from shelf-stable ingredients—that can be swapped when life throws unexpected challenges. These backup meals had saved me from expensive takeout orders countless times when meetings ran late or energy levels were low.

As you develop your meal-planning routine, create a master list of your household's favorite meals, categorized by preparation time and main ingredients. This resource becomes invaluable when you're short on planning time or inspiration. My list started with just ten reliable recipes and has grown to include dozens of options, each noted with approximate costs and preparation times.

Don't forget to consider your schedule when planning meals. Plan simpler meals or intentional leftovers on days with evening commitments or early meetings the next morning. I mark these schedule constraints directly on my meal plan, which helps ensure I'm not attempting an elaborate recipe on a day when time will be tight.

Finally, treat your first few weeks of meal planning as a learning experience. Keep notes about what worked well and what didn't, including preparation times, portion sizes, and family feedback. These insights will help you refine your approach and create more effective plans in the future. Remember, the goal isn't perfection - creating a sustainable system that works for your lifestyle and budget.

❦

Kitchen Organization Systems: Maximizing Space and Efficiency

My kitchen organization journey began with 'The Great Container Chaos' - a moment when I couldn't find the lid to a pot while dinner was threatening to boil over. That evening, after cleaning up a messy spill, I realized that an organized kitchen isn't just about aesthetics - it's about efficiency, safety, and saving time and money.

The foundation of an efficient kitchen lies in creating distinct work zones. I divide my kitchen into five key areas: food storage, preparation, cooking, cleaning, and serving. Each zone should contain everything needed for its specific function. For instance, my preparation zone includes cutting boards, knives, and measuring tools, all within arm's reach of my main counter space.

Here are the essential zones every budget-friendly kitchen needs:

- **Preparation Zone:** Main counter space, cutting boards, knives, measuring tools

- **Cooking Zone:** Stove, essential pots and pans, cooking utensils, spices

- **Storage Zone:** Pantry items, storage containers, food wraps

- **Cleaning Zone:** Sink, dish soap, cleaning supplies, trash bin

- **Serving Zone:** Plates, utensils, serving dishes

Essential Zones for a Budget-Friendly Kitchen

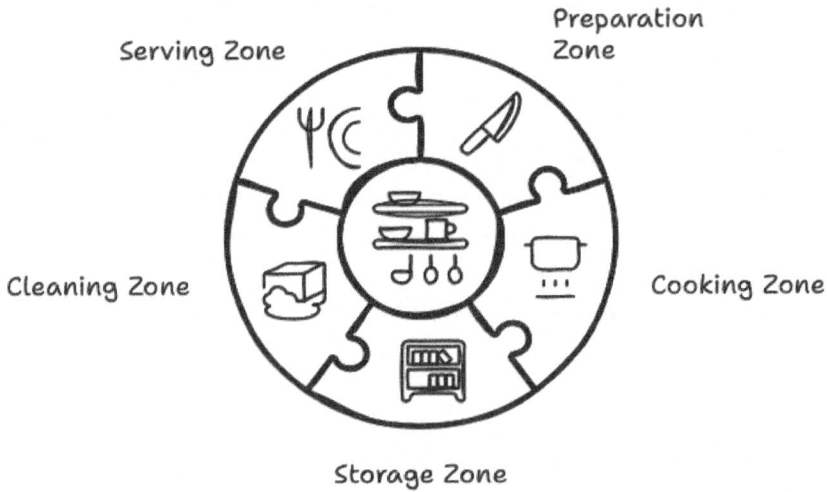

The magic happens when you organize these zones based on your cooking workflow. I learned to position frequently used items at eye level and within easy reach while storing seasonal or specialty items in higher or lower cabinets. This simple adjustment reduced my cooking time by nearly 20% and made meal preparation far more enjoyable.

Vertical space is often overlooked in kitchen organization, but it's a game-changer for small kitchens. I installed an inexpensive pegboard on one wall to hang frequently used pots and pans, freeing up valuable cabinet space. Command hooks inside cabinet doors now hold measuring cups and spoons, making them easily accessible without taking up drawer space.

One of my most effective organization strategies became my 'Clear Container Revolution.' After losing countless ingredients to the back of dark cabinets, I invested in clear storage containers. Now, I can instantly see what I have and how much remains. I label each container with contents and purchase date, dramatically reducing food waste and preventing duplicate purchases.

Cabinet organization doesn't require expensive solutions. I use repurposed shoe boxes as drawer dividers and old magazine holders to vertically organize cutting boards and baking sheets. These simple solutions cost nothing but save valuable space and make items more accessible. I created a two-tier system for spices using a simple shelf riser, allowing me to see all spice containers at once rather than hunting through a jumbled cabinet.

The refrigerator deserves special attention in any kitchen organization system. I establish clear zones here, too: ready-to-eat foods on top shelves, raw ingredients below, and produce in designated drawers. This promotes food safety and helps track what needs to be used first. I keep a whiteboard on the fridge listing perishable items and their use-by dates, significantly reducing food waste.

Counter space is precious in any kitchen, especially with a tight budget. I follow the 'prime real estate' rule: only items used daily earn a spot on the counter. My coffee maker and knife block stay out while the stand mixer lives in a cabinet. This keeps counters clear for meal prep and makes cleaning easier. A small tension rod under the sink creates vertical storage for cleaning sprays, freeing up valuable floor space.

One of my favorite space-saving solutions is the 'nested storage' approach. Mixing bowls, measuring cups, and food storage containers are nested together, maximizing vertical space. I keep the lids organized in a separate file organizer, eliminating the frustration of searching for matching pieces.

Remember that kitchen organization is an evolving process. Start with one zone or area that causes the most frustration and gradually work through the space. Pay attention to your cooking patterns and adjust your organization accordingly. What works for someone else might not work for you - the key is creating a system that supports your cooking style and budget goals.

I maintain my organized kitchen with a '2-minute rule': if something takes less than two minutes to put away correctly, do it immediately. This prevents the gradual chaos that can overtake even the best-organized spaces. Every few months, I reassess my zones and storage solutions, making adjustments based on seasonal needs or changes in cooking habits.

The actual test of any kitchen organization system is how well it supports your cooking goals. An organized kitchen should make cooking easier, stick to your meal plan, and maintain your budget. When everything has its place and is easily accessible, you're more likely to cook at home and less likely to resort to expensive takeout options. Remember, the goal isn't perfection - creating a functional space that makes both budget-friendly cooking easier and more enjoyable. As we conclude this foundational chapter, let's reflect on the essential building blocks we've explored to create a budget-friendly kitchen that works for you. My journey from poorly stored pasta to discovering the power of proper storage solutions shows how small kitchen organization and planning changes can lead to significant savings.

Through each section, we've built a comprehensive framework for success in budget meal planning. We started with the essential tools, proving that a well-equipped kitchen doesn't require endless gadgets – just thoughtfully chosen, multipurpose items that earn their keep. We explored building and maintaining a strategic pantry system that is the backbone of efficient, economical cooking. The smart shopping fundamentals we covered will help you navigate different store types and decide where to spend your grocery budget. By mastering basic meal planning techniques and kitchen organization, you can transform your kitchen into an efficient workspace that supports your budget-friendly cooking goals.

Remember that building a budget-friendly kitchen is a journey, not a destination. Start with the basics we've covered – proper storage solutions, essential tools, and simple organization systems – and build from there. Focus on creating sustainable habits that work for your lifestyle and space. Whether cooking for one in a tiny apartment or feeding a family in a spacious kitchen, these fundamental principles will help you maximize savings and efficiency.

As you progress, don't feel pressured to implement everything immediately. Choose one area to focus on: organizing your pantry, creating
your first meal plan, or streamlining your shopping routine. Small, consistent changes often lead to the most sustainable results. Remember my
learning curve with bulk buying and storage solutions – sometimes, our
mistakes become our best teachers.

In the chapters ahead, we'll build upon these fundamentals as we explore specific cooking techniques, recipe scaling, and creative ways to
maintain variety while staying within your budget. The foundation you've
built in this chapter – understanding essential tools, innovative shopping
strategies, meal planning basics, and kitchen organization – will support
all your future budget cooking endeavours.

Your journey to budget-friendly cooking starts with these fundamentals but doesn't end here. As you practice these principles and make them
your own, you'll discover that a well-organized, thoughtfully equipped
kitchen isn't just about saving money – it's about creating a space where
cooking becomes enjoyable and economical. Take these lessons forward
with you as we explore more advanced strategies and techniques in the
chapters ahead.

※》》》》 《《《《※

Chapter Two

Smart Shopping Strategies

Maximizing Value at Every Store Type

Like many shoppers, I initially felt stressed by the many choices and the need to make smart purchases while staying on budget. I learned how to navigate different types of stores and recognize their unique benefits. This knowledge has been essential for me as I work on cooking on a budget. my weekly shopping trips from stress-inducing marathons into efficient, money-saving missions. Like many shoppers, I initially felt overwhelmed by the seemingly endless choices and the challenge of making smart purchasing decisions while staying within my budget. Learning to navigate different store types and understand their unique advantages became crucial in my journey toward budget-conscious cooking.

Choose the best store type for maximizing shopping value.

Traditional Supermarkets
Offer a wide range of products and brand options

Discount Grocers
Focus on cost savings and budget-friendly options

I discovered that each type of store - from traditional supermarkets to discount grocers, warehouse clubs, and farmers markets - offers distinct opportunities for savings when approached with the right strategy. Understanding these differences transformed my shopping from a stressful guessing game into a systematic approach to maximizing value.

During my early days of budget shopping, I made the '$200 Impulse Mistake.' I had spotted what seemed like an incredible deal on bulk packages of chicken at a warehouse store and, without checking unit prices or considering my storage capacity, loaded my cart with enough meat to feed a small army. Back home, I realized my apartment freezer could only accommodate half of my purchase. In a panic, I called three friends to split the haul but lost some to freezer burn because I hadn't adequately portioned or stored the meat. This expensive lesson taught me the importance of strategic shopping - checking unit prices, considering storage space, and planning purchases based on actual needs rather than apparent deals. Now, I keep a small notebook with standard unit prices from different stores, helping me quickly identify genuine bargains and make informed decisions about where to shop for specific items. This system has saved me countless dollars and prevented food waste, turning me from an impulsive buyer into a savvy shopper.

In this chapter, We'll explore the essential strategies for making the most of different store types, from understanding store layouts to mastering unit pricing and loyalty programs. You'll learn how to evaluate store brands versus name brands, make informed decisions about bulk purchases, and navigate seasonal shopping opportunities. Whether shopping at a high-end supermarket or a discount store, these techniques will help you maximize your food budget while maintaining quality and nutrition.

Perhaps most importantly, you'll discover that smart shopping isn't about finding the cheapest option - it's about finding the best value for your needs and circumstances. By the end of this chapter, you'll have the confidence and knowledge to make strategic shopping decisions that support your financial goals and dietary preferences.

❧ ❦

Understanding Store Layouts and Psychology: Navigation Strategies for Maximum Savings

Have you ever noticed how grocery stores seem designed to lead you through a maze of tempting displays and strategic product placements? I constantly fell prey to these carefully orchestrated layouts during my early budget-conscious shopping days, often leaving the store with items I hadn't planned to buy. That was until I learned to decode the psychology behind store layouts and developed strategies to navigate them effectively.

Most grocery stores follow a predictable pattern - essential items like fresh produce, dairy, and meat are typically positioned around the store's perimeter. This isn't just for practical refrigeration; it's a deliberate strategy to guide shoppers through the entire store, exposing them to more products. Understanding this layout is your first step toward strategic shopping.

Here are the key zones you'll encounter and how to navigate them wisely:

How to navigate the grocery store for smart shopping?

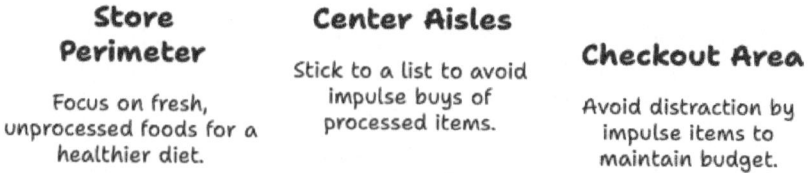

Store Perimeter

Focus on fresh, unprocessed foods for a healthier diet.

Center Aisles

Stick to a list to avoid impulse buys of processed items.

Checkout Area

Avoid distraction by impulse items to maintain budget.

Store Perimeter: Contains fresh departments like produce, meat, and dairy. Focus your shopping here for whole, unprocessed foods.

Center Aisles: Home to shelf-stable items and processed foods. Shop with a list to avoid impulse purchases.

Checkout Area: Filled with impulse items. Keep your eyes on your cart, not the candy display.

One of my most effective discoveries was the power of shopping 'backward' through the store. Instead of following the traditional counter-clockwise flow, I started entering through the rightmost aisle and working my way left. This simple change helped me avoid the carefully crafted path to maximize impulse purchases. I found myself spending less time in the store and sticking more closely to my shopping list.

Time of day also plays a crucial role in strategic shopping. Early mornings often offer the freshest produce and best meat selections, while evening shopping can yield discounts on perishable items. I learned this lesson one evening when I discovered my store's routine of marking down fresh items at 7PM - a timing insight that has saved me hundreds of dollars on high-quality proteins and produce.

Product placement within aisles follows its psychology. The most profitable items are typically placed at eye level, while better values can often be found on lower or higher shelves. I make it a habit to scan all shelf levels before selecting, often finding significant savings on identical products simply by looking up or down.

- **Look high and low:** Premium-priced items are usually at eye level

- **Check end caps carefully:** While they may feature sales, they don't always offer the best value

- **Avoid special displays:** Free-standing displays often feature standard-priced items in prime locations

Another crucial strategy is understanding the store's restocking schedule. Most stores restock shelves during off-peak hours, typically late evening or early morning. Shopping during or shortly after restocking means better selection and often first access to marked-down items. I've made it a habit to ask friendly staff about these schedules - information that has helped me consistently access the freshest products at the best prices.

The most valuable lesson I've learned is maintaining focus while shopping. I treat my grocery trips like strategic missions rather than casual browsing sessions. With my organized list in hand, grouped by store layout sections, I move purposefully through the store, avoiding the tempting displays and end-cap promotions that don't align with my planned purchases.

Remember, every store layout aspect is intentionally designed to encourage spending. From placing popular items deep within the store to carefully curated impulse buying sections, understanding these psychological tactics is your first defence against overspending. You can control your purchases and budget by approaching your shopping with awareness and a clear strategy.

The key to successful navigation isn't about avoiding all the store's marketing strategies - it's about recognizing them and making conscious choices about when and how to engage with them. This awareness, combined with purposeful shopping patterns, transforms your grocery trips from potential budget-busters into opportunities for significant savings.

⋙ ⋘

Comparing Store Types: When to Shop Where for Best Value

My journey to understanding different store types began with a spreadsheet and a month-long experiment tracking prices across various retailers. What I discovered transformed my shopping habits and revolutionized my food budget. Each type of store offers unique advantages, and knowing when to shop where can significantly impact your grocery spending.

Traditional supermarkets remain the cornerstone of grocery shopping, offering convenience and variety. However, I've learned they're best utilized for specific purposes. These stores excel at providing fresh produce, dairy, and meat when on sale, particularly during weekly specials. Their regular prices tend to be higher than discount alternatives, so I primarily use them for loss-leader sales (deeply discounted items used to draw customers in) and items I can't find elsewhere.

Discount grocery stores have become my go-to for pantry staples and everyday essentials. These stores offer 20-30% lower prices than traditional supermarkets by focusing on store brands and maintaining no-frills store environments. While the selection may be more limited, the quality of store-brand products often matches or exceeds that of national brands. These stores are particularly valuable for non-perishable items, basic produce, and dairy products.

Here are the key store types and their best uses.

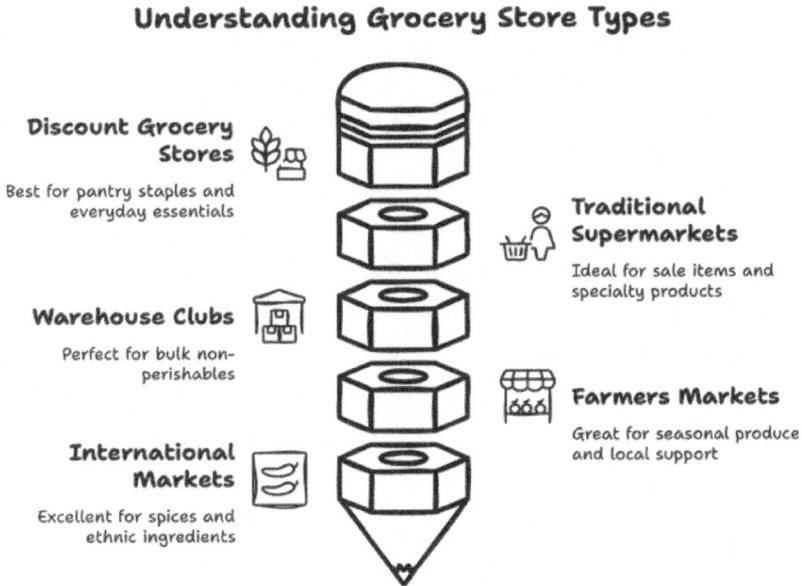

Understanding Grocery Store Types

Discount Grocery Stores
Best for pantry staples and everyday essentials

Traditional Supermarkets
Ideal for sale items and specialty products

Warehouse Clubs
Perfect for bulk non-perishables

Farmers Markets
Great for seasonal produce and local support

International Markets
Excellent for spices and ethnic ingredients

One of my most valuable discoveries was the power of **international markets** for specific categories. These stores often offer spices, rice, and legumes at a fraction of supermarket prices. During one shopping trip, I found a pound of cumin for the same price as a small jar at my regular grocery store - a discovery that prompted me to create a 'spice route' shopping map for my area.

Understanding their pricing cycles and sales patterns is the key to maximizing value across different store types. Traditional supermarkets typically operate on a 6-8 week sale cycle, while discount stores maintain more consistent pricing. I keep a price book noting the lowest prices for commonly purchased items at each store type, helping me recognize genuine deals when they appear.

Warehouse clubs deserve special consideration in your shopping strategy. While their bulk pricing can offer significant savings, I learned through experience that these savings only materialize if you can properly store and use the quantities purchased. After my chicken-buying mishap, I developed a simple rule: I only buy bulk items I use at least twice a month and have proper storage space.

Seasonal shopping adds another layer to store selection. **Farmers markets** often offer the best value for in-season produce, particularly during peak harvest times. Visiting near closing time can yield additional savings as vendors look to sell the remaining inventory. However, knowing your local growing seasons and typical prices are essential to recognize actual values.

Digital tools and **apps** have become invaluable allies in comparing stores and tracking prices. I use them to check prices across multiple stores before making my shopping plans, but I'm careful to factor in the cost of travel between locations. Sometimes, paying slightly more at one store proves more economical than driving to multiple locations.

The art of knowing where to shop extends beyond just price comparison. Quality, convenience, and time management are crucial in the value equation. I've learned to balance these factors by concentrating my shopping at two to three primary stores that consistently offer the best overall value for my needs, supplementing with occasional visits to specialty stores for specific items.

Remember that the 'best value' doesn't always mean the lowest price. Consider factors like food quality, shopping experience, and time investment when choosing where to shop. A slightly higher price at a store with better quality produce may represent a better value if it means less food waste in the long run.

Unit Pricing Mastery: Making Smart Price Comparisons

One of my most eye-opening moments in budget shopping came when I discovered I had been paying nearly twice as much for oatmeal simply because I hadn't understood unit pricing. Standing in the cereal aisle, comparing a small container of quick oats to a larger package, I finally took the time to calculate the cost per ounce. This simple math revealed that I was paying a premium for convenience packaging rather than the product.

Unit pricing is your secret weapon for making smart purchasing decisions. It compares products based on their cost per unit of measurement (like ounces, pounds, or sheets) rather than the total package price. This standardized comparison helps you identify the actual value of products regardless of package size or marketing presentation.

Essential steps for mastering unit pricing:

- Look for the unit price label on store shelves (usually shown as price per ounce or pound)

- If not displayed, divide the total price by the number of units (usually shown as price per ounce or pound)

- Compare similar products using the same unit of measurement

- Consider storage capacity and usage rates alongside unit price

- Watch for deceptive packaging that may hide actual unit costs

---

Learning to calculate unit prices quickly became second nature, but I still remember the **simple formula: total price divided by total units equals price per unit.** For example, if a 16-ounce jar of sauce costs \$3.20, the unit price is $0.20 per ounce ($3.20 ÷ 16 = $0.20). This basic math has saved me countless dollars over the years.

One common misconception I encountered was that larger packages always offer better value. While this is often true, it's not universal. I've frequently found mid-sized packages offering better unit prices than bulk options, especially during sales. This discovery taught me always to check unit prices regardless of package size.

The real power of unit pricing comes into play when comparing different brands and package sizes. For instance, I once compared three different sizes of rice: a 1-pound bag, a 5-pound bag, and a 20-pound bag. While the 20-pound bag had the lowest unit price, storing such a large quantity in my apartment wasn't practical. This taught me that the best unit price isn't always the best choice – storage capacity, usage rate, and food freshness must also factor into the decision.

Different product categories require different unit pricing strategies. Since storage life isn't a concern, buying the lowest unit price often makes sense for non-perishables like paper products or canned goods. However, the lowest unit price for perishables might lead to waste if you can't use the product before it spoils. I learned this lesson the hard way with a large bag of apples that offered an excellent unit price but led to waste when I couldn't eat them all in time.

Key considerations when applying unit pricing:

- **Storage capacity and shelf life** of products

- Your **typical usage rate** for the item

- **Seasonal price** fluctuations

- **Quality** differences between brands

- **Additional costs** like storage containers or freezer bags

---

Digital tools have made unit price calculations more straightforward than ever. While many stores now display unit prices on shelf labels, I keep a basic calculator handy for unique displays or farmer's market purchases where unit prices aren't shown. Some grocery store apps even include unit price comparisons, though I've found it valuable to know how to calculate these manually as a backup.

The most valuable lesson I've learned about unit pricing is that it's not just about finding the lowest price – it's about finding the best value for your situation. Sometimes, paying a slightly higher unit price for a smaller package makes more sense if it prevents waste or better fits your storage capacity. The key is using unit pricing as one tool in your broader shopping strategy, alongside considerations like quality, storage, and actual usage patterns.

Remember that unit prices can vary significantly between stores and seasons. I maintain a simple note on my phone with the typical unit prices of my most purchased items at different stores. This reference point helps me quickly identify genuine deals and make informed decisions about where to shop for specific items. Over time, this practice has helped me develop an intuitive sense of what constitutes good value in different product categories.

⤜⤛⤛ ⤜⤛⤜

Store Brand vs. Name Brand: Quality Assessment and Cost Analysis

One of my most transformative shopping revelations came during a blind taste test I conducted in my kitchen. Lined up on my counter were two sets of basic pantry staples - one name brand, one store brand - ranging from canned tomatoes to breakfast cereals. With the help of my notebook and an honest palate, I discovered something that would forever change my shopping habits. In many cases, I couldn't tell the difference between store brands and their pricier counterparts.

The relationship between stores and name brands is more complex than many shoppers realize. Store brands, also known as private label products, are often manufactured in the same facilities as name brands, sometimes even using identical recipes. The primary difference? Marketing costs and brand premiums can increase prices by 20-30%.

Key categories where **store brands typically offer excellent value:**
- Pantry staples (flour, sugar, salt)

- Canned goods and basic condiments

- Dairy products and eggs

- Basic frozen vegetables

- Paper products and cleaning supplies

However, not all store brands are created equal. Through systematic testing and comparison, I've learned to evaluate store brands in three crucial areas: ingredient quality, taste, and performance consistency. This approach has helped me identify which store brand products offer genuine value versus those where the name brand superiority justifies the higher cost.

My evaluation process begins with an ingredient comparison. I carefully examine labels for main ingredients, additives, and nutritional content differences. Often, I find store brands match their name-brand counterparts almost precisely. However, there are exceptions - particularly in products where ingredient quality significantly impacts the final result, like chocolate chips for baking or certain condiments.

The cost savings from choosing store brands can be substantial. During my first month of intentionally switching to store brands where appropriate, I tracked every purchase and discovered I had reduced my grocery bill by nearly 15% without sacrificing quality. This amounted to about $60 in savings - money I could reinvest in higher-quality ingredients for recipes where brand names made a difference.

One particularly successful strategy I've developed is the 'progressive testing' approach. Instead of switching all products to store brands at once, I test one category at a time, giving myself time to evaluate the results in real-world cooking situations. This methodical approach helped me build confidence in in-store brand products while identifying the few categories where name brands outperformed their cheaper counterparts.

Here are some guidelines for effective brand comparison.

Navigating Brand Comparisons Effectively

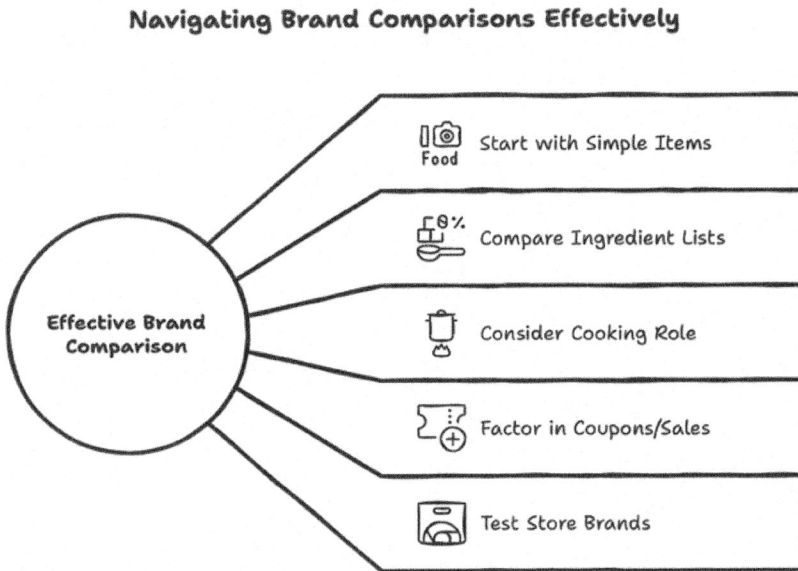

Effective Brand Comparison

- Start with Simple Items
- Compare Ingredient Lists
- Consider Cooking Role
- Factor in Coupons/Sales
- Test Store Brands

Quality assessment goes beyond just taste and price. I've learned to consider packaging quality, storage life, and product consistency. Some store brands may offer significant savings but require better storage solutions or faster use to maintain quality. Understanding these trade-offs helps make informed decisions about when to choose store versus name brands.

One surprising discovery was that store brand quality can vary significantly between retailers. A store brand product from one supermarket chain might be excellent, while the same type of product from another chain could be disappointing. I keep notes on these differences in my shopping journal, helping me remember which stores offer the best private-label options in different categories.

The most valuable lesson about store brands is that brand loyalty should be based on experience rather than marketing or assumptions. Some of my favorite products now are store brands I initially approached with scepticism. By remaining open-minded and systematic in my evaluation process, I've found a balance that maximizes both quality and value in my shopping.

Remember that the goal isn't to eliminate name brands but to identify where store brands offer equivalent quality at better prices. This knowledge allows you to allocate your food budget more effectively, spending more on items where brand names truly matter while saving on products where store brands perform just as well

⋙⋙⋙ ⋘⋘⋘

Digital Tools and Loyalty Programs: Maximizing Modern Shopping Benefits

My introduction to digital shopping tools came through watching my grocery bill steadily climb during a particularly tight month. I discovered I had been missing hundreds of dollars in savings by not utilizing the digital tools available at my regular grocery store. That weekend, I sat down and systematically explored every feature of my store's app, uncovering a world of digital coupons, personalized deals, and loyalty program benefits I had been overlooking.

Modern grocery shopping has evolved far beyond paper coupons and punch cards. Today's digital tools and loyalty programs offer sophisticated ways to maximize savings while streamlining the shopping experience. The key is effectively integrating these tools into your shopping routine without letting them dictate your buying decisions.

Here are the essential digital tools every budget-conscious shopper should consider.

Tools

Meal planning apps

Store-specific shopping apps

Digital loyalty program trackers

Price comparison apps

Receipt scanning apps

One of the most valuable lessons I've learned is the importance of strategic loyalty program participation. While joining every program available is tempting, focusing on the stores where I shop most frequently is more effective. I maintain active involvement in three primary loyalty programs, which allows me to maximize benefits without spreading my spending too thin across multiple stores.

The real power of digital tools comes from their integration. For example, I discovered that by linking my store's loyalty card to their app, I could automatically access personalized deals based on my shopping history. These deals often align with items I regularly purchase, creating additional savings on products I would buy anyway. This systematic approach to digital savings has reduced my monthly grocery bill by approximately 20% without changing my shopping habits.

However, it's crucial to approach digital tools and loyalty programs with a strategic mindset. Just because an app offers a discount doesn't mean the item is the best value or something you need. I maintain a simple rule: I only use digital coupons for items already on my shopping list or staples I know We'll use. This prevents the common trap of buying something solely because it's on sale.

Key strategies for maximizing loyalty program benefits:
- **Stack digital coupons** with store sales when possible

- **Track reward point expiration dates**

- Focus on **programs offering cash back or store credit** rather than points

- Review **digital offers** before **making your shopping list**

- Consider **seasonal bonus point** opportunities

One particularly effective strategy or digital deal stacking involves combining store sales, digital coupons, and loyalty program rewards to maximize savings on a single purchase. For example, I once purchased my favorite brand of coffee when it was on sale, used a digital coupon from the store's app, and earned bonus loyalty points during a special promotion. This combination resulted in a 60% savings on a product I buy regularly.

The key to successful digital tool usage is organization. I dedicate fifteen minutes each week to reviewing available digital coupons, checking loyalty program rewards, and updating my shopping list accordingly. This systematic approach ensures I don't miss valuable savings opportunities while preventing the overwhelming feeling that can come from managing multiple apps and programs.

Remember that digital tools should serve your shopping strategy, not drive it. While these resources can offer significant savings, they should complement your budget meal planning rather than dictate your purchases. I've learned to view digital tools as enhancers of my shopping strategy rather than its foundation.

Protect your privacy while using digital tools. I maintain a separate email address for shopping accounts and carefully review privacy settings in shopping apps. This allows me to benefit from digital savings while controlling my personal information.

The digital shopping landscape continues to evolve, with new tools and features regularly becoming available. Stay informed about updates to your preferred store's app and loyalty program, but don't feel pressured to adopt every new feature. Focus on the tools that provide genuine value for your shopping habits and budget goals. As we conclude our exploration of innovative shopping strategies, it's worth reflecting on how understanding store layouts, mastering unit pricing, and leveraging digital tools can transform your grocery shopping from a budget strain into an opportunity for significant savings. Through my journey from overwhelmed shopper to strategic saver, I've learned that successful budget shopping isn't about finding the cheapest options but maximizing value through informed decisions and systematic approaches.

The lessons we've covered in this chapter - from navigating different store types to evaluating store brands against name brands - provide a foundation for smarter shopping habits. These strategies become even more valuable in today's economic climate, where making informed choices can significantly impact your food budget. Remember that successful budget shopping is a skill that develops over time, building on small victories and learning from occasional missteps like my own '$200 Impulse Mistake.'

Start small as you begin applying these techniques in your shopping routine. Consider beginning with unit price comparisons in one product category or experimenting with store brands for essential pantry items. Pay attention to store layouts and test different shopping patterns to find what works best. Most importantly, remember that every shopping trip is an opportunity to refine your approach and build confidence in your decision-making.

The digital tools and loyalty programs we discussed can amplify your savings, but they should support rather than drive your shopping strategy. Focus on developing a strong foundation in the basics - understanding store layouts, mastering unit pricing, and making informed brand choices. These fundamental skills will serve you well regardless of which stores you shop at or which digital tools you use.

Remember that successful budget shopping isn't about deprivation - it's about making informed choices that align with your financial goals and food preferences. By applying the strategies we've discussed, you can maintain quality while reducing costs, creating a sustainable approach to grocery shopping that supports your overall budget meal planning goals.

As you move forward, keep building your knowledge of local stores, refining your price awareness, and staying flexible. The most successful budget shoppers can adapt their strategies as circumstances change while maintaining their commitment to value-based decisions. In the next chapter, we'll build on these shopping fundamentals as we explore the art of batch cooking for small households, where these innovative shopping strategies become the foundation for efficient meal preparation.

Chapter Three

The Art of Batch Cooking

Small-Scale Success for Solo Cooks

My tiny apartment kitchen felt like an impossible space for batch cooking until I discovered the power of strategic planning and creative container solutions. Like solving a puzzle, I learned to transform my limited counter space and modest freezer into an efficient batch cooking command center that saved time and money. As I discovered through trial and error, batch cooking doesn't require expansive counter space or industrial-sized appliances - it just demands thoughtful planning and creative solutions. The cramped quarters of my urban apartment became my testing ground for developing small-scale batch cooking techniques that would revolutionize how I approached meal preparation.

Batch cooking, often associated with large families or meal prep businesses, can be just as valuable for solo cooks and small households. It's about balancing quantity and practicality, saving time and maintaining variety. Through careful portioning and strategic storage, even those cooking for one can harness the time-saving benefits of batch preparation while avoiding the dreaded meal fatigue that often comes with eating the same dish multiple times.

I learned lessons from my first batch of cooking attempts in my tiny apartment. Armed with multiple recipes and countless ingredients, I ambitiously prepared a month's worth of meals in one day. I quickly realized I had severely underestimated the spatial challenges of my kitchen. Containers overflowed my limited counter space, and I discovered my freezer could barely hold a quarter of what I'd prepared. In a moment of panic, with cooling food everywhere and no place to store it, I had to innovate quickly. Using my bed as an extra cooling station and my living room coffee table as a prep area, I completed the marathon cooking session.

This chaotic experience taught me valuable lessons about scaling appropriately for my space and the importance of planning storage solutions before starting any batch cooking project. Now, I approach batch cooking with a well-thought-out strategy, focusing on preparing 3 to 4 base recipes that can be transformed into various meals, using stackable containers that maximize my limited freezer space, and scheduling shorter, more manageable cooking sessions that don't overwhelm my kitchen.

In this chapter, we'll explore how to master the art of small-scale batch cooking, from selecting the right recipes to scale down, maximizing limited storage space, and maintaining food quality during storage. You'll learn how to transform your kitchen, regardless of size, into an efficient batch-cooking command center that saves time and money. Whether you're cooking for yourself or a small household, these techniques will help you embrace the benefits of batch cooking while avoiding its common pitfalls.

Scaling Down Recipes: Converting Family-Sized Portions to Solo Servings

One of my earliest kitchen challenges was adapting my grandmother's beloved lasagna recipe that served twelve down to single portions. After several attempts that left me eating the same lasagna for weeks, I discovered that successfully scaling down recipes requires more than simple division - it demands an understanding of ingredient relationships and cooking dynamics.

The first step in scaling down recipes is understanding that not all ingredients scale linearly. While dividing everything by the same number is tempting, some ingredients like herbs, spices, and cooking times need special consideration. I realized this when I reduced the garlic in a recipe and found the dish to be noticeably under-seasoned. Now, I use a '2/3 rule' for spices and seasonings - when cutting a recipe in half, I use about two-thirds of the original amount of seasonings rather than half.

- Start with simple recipes that have easily divisible measurements

- Use measuring tools designed for smaller portions (quarter cups, half tablespoons)

- Consider investing in smaller cooking vessels suited for individual portions

- Keep a conversion chart handy for quick reference

- Write down successful adjustments for future use

When scaling down recipes, cooking times and temperatures often need adjustment. A casserole scaled down from a 9x13 inch pan to an 8x8 inch pan may cook faster and require a slightly lower temperature to prevent burning. I discovered this when my scaled-down shepherd's pie developed a too-crispy top while the center remained cool. When significantly scaling down a recipe, I typically reduce cooking time and temperature by about 25%.

Equipment selection plays a crucial role in successful recipe scaling. While my full-sized lasagna required a large baking dish, attempting to make a single portion in the same pan would result in a too-thin, likely overcooked dish. I've built a collection of smaller baking dishes, ramekins, and mini loaf pans that help maintain proper ingredient ratios and cooking dynamics when preparing scaled-down recipes.

Storage solutions become equally important when cooking smaller portions. Rather than struggling with oversized storage containers that waste valuable fridge space, I use a variety of small, stackable containers that better fit individual portions. This maximizes storage space, helps maintain food quality, and prevents waste.

- Small ramekins (4-6 oz) for individual casseroles and baked dishes

- Mini loaf pans for scaled-down breads and meatloaves

- 8x8 inch baking dishes for quarter-sized batch recipes

- Individual-sized storage containers with tight-fitting lids

- Silicone muffin cups for portioning and freezing

One beneficial strategy I've developed is the 'base recipe' approach. Instead of scaling down complete recipes, I prepare basic components that can be used in multiple ways. For example, a basic tomato sauce can become pasta sauce one night, pizza topping another, and part of a casserole later in the week. This approach provides variety while maintaining the efficiency of batch cooking.

I've found several workable solutions when scaling down recipes that call for eggs, which can be tricky to divide. For recipes calling for one egg in the original, I either use the yolk or just the white depending on the recipe's purpose (yolks for richness, whites for structure), or I beat the egg and measure out half. The remaining egg can be stored in a small container and used within 24 hours for another scaled recipe or breakfast.

Perhaps most importantly, I've learned to be flexible and creative when scaling down recipes. Sometimes, exact division isn't possible or practical, and that's okay. The goal is to maintain the spirit and flavor of the original recipe while adapting it to serve your needs. Keep notes on what works and what doesn't, and don't be afraid to adjust based on your preferences and experiences.

- Document successful adaptations in a dedicated notebook

- Note any adjustments to cooking times and temperatures

- Record substitutions that worked well

- Keep track of preferred portion sizes

- Make notes about storage methods and shelf life

Scaling down recipes successfully takes practice and patience, but the reward is enjoying various meals without waste or repetition. Remember that cooking is both a science and an art - while precise measurements matter, there's room for creativity and personal preference in the scaling process.

Strategic Prep Sessions: Organizing Your Small-Space Batch Cooking

The key to successful batch cooking in a small space is treating your kitchen like a professional chef's station - every movement and surface area must be purposeful and efficient. When I first started batch cooking in my tiny apartment kitchen, I often danced an awkward shuffle between the stove and counter, desperately searching for space to put down a hot pot or trying to find my measuring spoons buried under prep bowls. Through trial and error, I developed a systematic approach that transformed my cramped cooking space into an efficient prep station.

Kitchen Organization Strategy

The foundation of strategic prep sessions starts with creating distinct zones in your kitchen. I designate specific areas for different tasks: a prep zone for chopping and measuring, a cooking zone near the stove, and a cooling zone for finished dishes. Even in my modest kitchen, I've learned to maximize vertical space by using stackable cooling racks and utilizing the top of my refrigerator as additional storage during prep sessions.

- Clear counters completely before starting

- Set up a dedicated chopping station with a cutting board and knife

- Create a 'mise en place' area for measured ingredients

- Designate a specific spot for cooling dishes

- Establish a cleaning station with a bowl of soapy water for quick cleanup

The success of a small-space batch cooking session relies heavily on planning. I create a sequence of tasks organized by cooking time and temperature requirements. This prevents bottlenecks and ensures efficient use of both time and space. For instance, while cooking rice, I can prep vegetables for multiple dishes, and while a casserole bakes, I can portion and package completed items.

One game-changing strategy I use utilizes a 'rolling prep'. Instead of preparing everything at once, I break down my batch of cooking into manageable waves. Each wave focuses on complementary dishes that can share prep work or cooking space. For example, if I'm making several dishes that require diced onions, I'll chop all the onions at once, portion them out, and then move on to the following shared ingredient.

- Group recipes by shared ingredients

- Organize tasks by cooking temperature and time

- Plan for overlapping cooking times

- Schedule cleanup breaks between waves

- Allow time for proper cooling before storage

Temperature management becomes crucial in small-space batch cooking. Without the luxury of sprawling counter space, you must be strategic about how and when you cool dishes. I use a combination of cooling racks and strategic placement to manage temperature efficiently. Hot dishes are placed near ventilation or open windows, while items requiring refrigeration are prepared last to minimize their time at room temperature.

The secret to successful small-space batch cooking lies in the knowledge and experience I have gained to maintain a continuous flow. Rather than letting dishes and utensils pile up, I incorporate cleaning and storing into the cooking process. A bowl of hot soapy water stays ready for quick washing between tasks, and storage containers are laid out and labeled before cooking begins. This prevents the dreaded end-of-session cleanup overwhelm and keeps the limited workspace functional throughout the process.

- Keep cleaning supplies easily accessible

- Wash tools and bowls between uses

- Label storage containers before filling

- Pack away completed dishes immediately

- Maintain a clear path to frequently used areas

Organization extends to ingredient management as well. I pre-measure all ingredients for each recipe and arrange them in groupings on a small rolling cart or tray. This mobile prep station can be moved around my kitchen, keeping ingredients accessible without cluttering valuable counter space. Inspired by professional kitchen practices, this method helps prevent the chaos of searching for ingredients mid-recipe.

The final piece of the small-space batch cooking puzzle is innovative storage solutions. I use a combination of stackable containers and vacuum-sealed bags to maximize freezer space. Each container is clearly labelled with contents and dates, and I maintain a simple inventory system to track what I have stored. This organization prevents forgotten freezer meals and helps maintain a rotation of different dishes to avoid meal fatigue.

Through these strategic approaches to batch cooking, I've learned that a small kitchen doesn't have to limit your meal prep ambitions. It's about working brighter, not more complicated, and treating your limited space as an opportunity to develop more efficient cooking habits. With proper planning and organization, even the smallest kitchen can become a productive batch cooking station that helps you save both time and money.

❦

Storage Solutions: Maximizing Limited Freezer and Fridge Space

Maximizing limited storage space became necessary when I moved into my first apartment with its modest refrigerator and tiny freezer compartment. Like many, I initially struggled with the Tetris-like challenge of fitting batch-cooked meals and fresh ingredients into confined spaces. Through experimentation and necessity, I developed a system that transformed my limited storage from frustration into a well-organized asset.

The foundation of efficient cold storage begins with proper container selection. After wasting money on mismatched containers that created precarious stacking situations, I invested in a set of uniform, stackable containers in various sizes. Square and rectangular containers became my go-to choices as they maximize space better than round ones and create more stable stacking arrangements. I also discovered the value of containers with measurement markings, which simplified portion control and ingredient prep.

Container selection
- Choose stackable containers with secure, leakproof lids

- Opt for square or rectangular shapes over round

- Select clear containers for easy content identification

- Invest in various sizes for different portion needs

- Look for freezer-safe materials that won't crack at low temperatures

---

I organize the refrigerator using a systematic approach. Each shelf has a designated purpose, with frequently used items at eye level and longer-lasting ingredients stored in lower sections. The door, being the warmest part of the fridge, holds condiments and other items that are less sensitive to temperature fluctuations. I maintain a 'first in, first out' rotation system, placing newer items behind older ones to prevent food waste.

In the freezer, vertical space becomes crucial. I use slim, stackable containers and freezer bags that can be stored upright like books on a shelf. Before freezing liquids like soups or sauces, I leave headspace in containers to allow for expansion. For items like herbs, stock, or sauce portions, I freeze them in ice cube trays first, then transfer them to freezer bags - a technique that allows me to use just what I need without thawing entire portions.

- Label everything with contents and date

- Store similar items together for easy access

- Use freezer bags for items that can be stored flat

- Implement a rotation system to prevent freezer burn

- Keep an inventory list on the freezer door

One of my most effective discoveries was the power of proper portioning before storage. Rather than storing large batches that require complete thawing, I divide meals into individual or two-person portions before freezing. This makes defrosting more manageable, helps maintain organization, and prevents waste from partially used containers.

Temperature management plays a crucial role in maximizing storage life. I keep a thermometer in both the refrigerator and freezer to ensure optimal temperatures - 40°F (4°C) or below for the fridge and 0°F (-18°C) or below for the freezer. I've learned to avoid overcrowding, as proper air circulation is essential for maintaining consistent temperatures and food safety.

I use a combination of produce bags and containers designed to extend shelf life for fresh produce storage. Leafy greens stay crisp longer when stored with a slightly damp paper towel, while herbs remain fresh in jars with a bit of water, covered loosely with plastic bags. Root vegetables find their home in the crisper drawer, separated from fruits that produce ethylene gas, which can speed up ripening.

- Use produce storage bags or containers designed for specific items

- Separate ethylene-producing fruits from sensitive vegetables

- Store herbs upright in water, like fresh flowers

- Keep potatoes and onions in cool, dark places outside the fridge

- Monitor moisture levels to prevent premature spoilage

The key to maintaining this system is regular inventory management. Each week, I dedicate a few minutes to checking expiration dates, rotating items, and updating my freezer inventory list. This practice prevents food waste and helps with meal planning and grocery shopping efficiency.

Perhaps most importantly, I've learned to resist the urge to overfill storage spaces. Maintaining open space in the refrigerator and freezer allows for better air circulation and makes accessing and organizing items easier. This discipline helps prevent forgotten items from languishing in the back of shelves and ensures that everything stored can be used efficiently.

These methods have transformed my limited storage space from a constraint into an advantage. The systems I've developed have helped me become more mindful of food usage and storage, leading to less waste and better organization. Remember, successful storage in small spaces isn't about fitting in as much as possible - it's about storing smartly and maintaining accessibility.

Base Recipe Variations: Creating Diverse Meals from Core Ingredients

The true power of batch cooking lies in preparing meals ahead of time and creating versatile base recipes that can transform into multiple distinct dishes. I discovered this principle during a particularly tight month when my grocery budget was stretched thin. Instead of viewing it as a limitation, I turned it into a creative challenge to see how many meals I could create from a single base recipe.

One of my most successful experiments began with a large batch of seasoned black beans. The first night, they served as a hearty bean and rice bowl. The next day, I transformed a portion into black bean soup by adding extra broth and different spices. Later in the week, those same beans became vegetarian tacos and a protein-rich addition to a colorful salad. Each meal felt distinct despite starting from the same base ingredient.

Preparing meals ahead
- Choose versatile base ingredients that work in multiple cuisines

- Master basic seasoning combinations that can be easily modified

- Plan complementary ingredients that can create different flavor profiles

- Consider texture variations to keep meals interesting

- Stock pantry items that can transform base recipes

The key to successful base recipe variations lies in a collection of shelf-stable ingredients that can quickly change the character of a dish. Different spice blends, canned tomatoes, coconut milk, and various grains become the building blocks for creating distinct meals from essential ingredients.

One of my favorite base recipes combines seasonal vegetables roasted with olive oil and basic seasonings. This foundation can become countless weekly meals: tossed with pasta and parmesan for an Italian dinner, added to curry sauce over rice for an Indian-inspired meal, or pureed into a creamy soup with broth and herbs.

Protein bases offer similar versatility. An essential shredded chicken preparation, seasoned simply with salt and pepper, can transform into chicken salad, enchiladas, soup, or stir-fry, depending on the additional ingredients and seasonings used. The key is to keep the base preparation neutral enough to work with various flavor profiles while ensuring it's properly cooked and seasoned.

- Prepare proteins with minimal seasoning to maintain flexibility

- Keep a variety of sauces and condiments on hand

- Learn basic sauce preparations that can transform dishes

- Stock frozen vegetables for quick additions

- Master the art of herb and spice combinations

Grains and legumes are excellent base recipes that stretch your budget while providing numerous meal possibilities. A large batch of quinoa can become a breakfast porridge with fruit and honey, a Mediterranean-style salad for lunch, or a stir-fry base for dinner. The same principle applies to lentils, rice, and other grains that can serve as neutral canvases for different flavor combinations.

The success of base recipe variations often depends on proper storage and reheating techniques. I portion base recipes in ways that make sense for their intended uses - some in meal-sized containers, others in smaller quantities for flexible use. Proper labeling becomes crucial, as does understanding how different ingredients hold up to various cooking methods.

Perhaps most importantly, I've learned to balance planning and flexibility. While I might start the week with specific transformations in mind, I remain open to creative inspiration based on what I'm craving or what additional ingredients I have. This approach prevents meal fatigue and helps reduce food waste by encouraging innovative use of ingredients.

- Keep a log of successful variations for future reference

- Note which combinations work best together

- Document cooking time adjustments for different variations

- Track which transformations maintain the best food quality

- Record family favorites for regular rotation

The art of creating diverse meals from core ingredients isn't just about saving money - it's about developing cooking confidence and creativity. Each successful variation builds your culinary intuition and expands your repertoire of possible meals. What starts as a practical solution to budget constraints often becomes a preferred cooking method, offering both efficiency and variety in your meal planning.

Quality Preservation: Proper Storage Techniques for Solo Portions

My journey into proper food storage began with a costly mistake that taught me the importance of correct storage techniques for single portions. After preparing a large batch of my favorite chicken stir-fry, I tossed the leftovers into a single large container and popped it in the freezer. A month later, I discovered a frost-covered mass that had lost its texture and flavor. This experience led me to develop a systematic approach to preserving quality in solo portions.

The foundation of quality preservation lies in understanding how different foods respond to storage. Proteins, vegetables, grains, and sauces each require specific handling to maintain their best qualities. I've learned that proper portioning, packaging, and temperature control are the three pillars of successful food storage for single servings.

Proper Storage Techniques

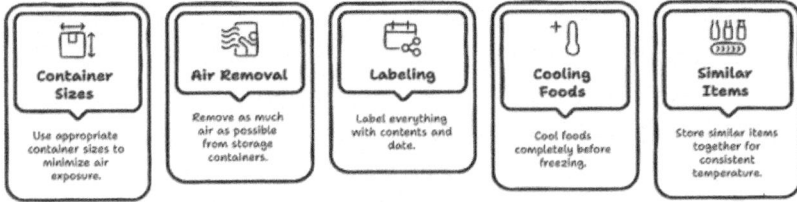

Container Sizes	Air Removal	Labeling	Cooling Foods	Similar Items
Use appropriate container sizes to minimize air exposure.	Remove as much air as possible from storage containers.	Label everything with contents and date.	Cool foods completely before freezing.	Store similar items together for consistent temperature.

One of the most crucial aspects of quality preservation is temperature control. Foods should be cooled quickly but safely to prevent bacterial growth while maintaining texture and flavor. I use a '2-Hour Rule' - getting foods from cooking temperature to storage temperature within two hours, using an ice bath when necessary to speed the process for more significant portions.

For freezer storage, portion size becomes critical. I've found that smaller portions freeze more quickly (which helps preserve quality) and thaw more evenly. I typically portion proteins in 4-6 ounce servings, vegetables in 1-cup portions, and grains in ½-cup servings. These sizes work well for single meals while allowing flexibility in combining different components.

Moisture control plays a vital role in maintaining food quality during storage. I use a quick blanching technique for vegetables, followed by thorough drying before freezing. This helps preserve colour, texture, and nutritional value. For cooked grains, I slightly undercook them when planning to freeze, as they'll absorb more moisture during reheating.

- Blanch vegetables before freezing to maintain quality

- Pat foods dry before freezing to prevent ice crystal formation

- Use moisture-barrier containers or bags

- Wrap foods tightly to prevent freezer burn

- Consider vacuum sealing for more extended storage

The type of container you use can significantly impact food quality during storage. I invest in high-quality, airtight containers specifically designed for freezer use. For items I plan to keep in the refrigerator, I use clear containers that allow me to monitor freshness. Glass containers with snap-locking lids have quickly become my favorite for both fridge and freezer storage, as they don't absorb odors or stains and can go directly from freezer to microwave.

Organizing stored foods properly helps maintain their quality and prevents waste. I use a first-in, first-out (FIFO) rotation system and keep an inventory list on my phone. This allows me to track what I have and when it needs to be used. I also organize my freezer into zones - one for proteins, one for vegetables, and one for prepared meals - making it easier to find items quickly and maintain proper temperature control.

Reheating stored foods properly is just as important as storing them correctly. I've developed specific reheating techniques for different types of foods to maintain their quality. For example, I thaw frozen proteins in the refrigerator overnight rather than using the microwave and add water when reheating grains to restore moisture.

- Thaw foods in the refrigerator whenever possible

- Use gentle reheating methods to prevent overcooking

- Add moisture back to foods as needed during reheating

- Let foods come to room temperature before reheating

- Use appropriate heat levels for different types of food

Perhaps most importantly, I've learned to be realistic about storage times. Even with perfect storage techniques, most foods have a limited freezer life before quality declines. I keep a chart on my freezer door with recommended storage times for different types of foods, helping me use items while they're at their best.

Through these methods, I've transformed my food storage from a hit-or-miss proposition into a reliable system that maintains quality while accommodating my single-portion needs. The key is treating food storage as an integral part of the cooking process, not an afterthought. When you take the time to store foods properly, you're not just preserving meals - you're maintaining their quality, flavor and investment in preparing them. As we conclude our exploration of small-scale batch cooking, it's clear that limited kitchen space need not limit your culinary ambitions or budget-saving goals. Even the tiniest kitchen can become an efficient meal preparation hub through strategic planning, creative storage solutions, and thoughtful recipe scaling. The journey from my chaotic first attempts at batch cooking to developing a streamlined system taught me that success lies not in the size of your kitchen but in how intelligently you use your space.

The key principles we've covered - from scaling down family recipes to maximizing storage space, from creating versatile base recipes to preserving food quality - form a comprehensive approach to small-scale batch cooking that can transform how you approach meal preparation. These techniques save money and time and ensure that cooking for one or two remains enjoyable and varied.

The most valuable lesson is that batch cooking for small households isn't about preparing enormous quantities of food or having industrial-sized storage space. Instead, it's about balancing efficiency and practicality, saving time and maintaining variety. By mastering these techniques, you can enjoy the benefits of batch cooking while avoiding common pitfalls like meal fatigue or food waste.

As you implement these strategies in your kitchen, remember that perfection isn't the goal - progress is. Start with simple recipes that are easy to scale, experiment with storage solutions that work for your space, and gradually build your confidence in creating varied meals from base recipes. With practice, you'll develop a personalized system that transforms your kitchen, regardless of size, into an efficient batch cooking command center that saves time and money.

Whether cooking in a compact apartment kitchen or working with limited storage space, our explored principles and techniques will help you maximize batch cooking while maintaining food quality and variety.

Remember, successful batch cooking for small households isn't about cooking more - it's about cooking smarter.

Chapter Four

Quick Prep, Big Savings

Time-Efficient Meal Solutions

Time is money, and nowhere is this more true than in the kitchen, where rushed evenings often lead to expensive takeout decisions. As I discovered during my journey from a time-stressed professional to an efficient home cook, the secret lies in cooking faster and wiser. Like most busy professionals, I learned this lesson the hard way. The path to more brilliant cooking began one evening during my busiest work period as I looked at my credit card statement and realized how much money I was losing to the convenience of takeout. I had fallen into the common trap of believing I didn't have time to cook when I needed to revolutionize my approach to meal preparation.

Time-efficient meal solutions

Pros	vs	Cons
🐷 Saves money		Initial effort
Healthier meals		Learning curve
Less stress		Potential for boredom
More free time		Requires organization
Better meal planning		Upfront cost

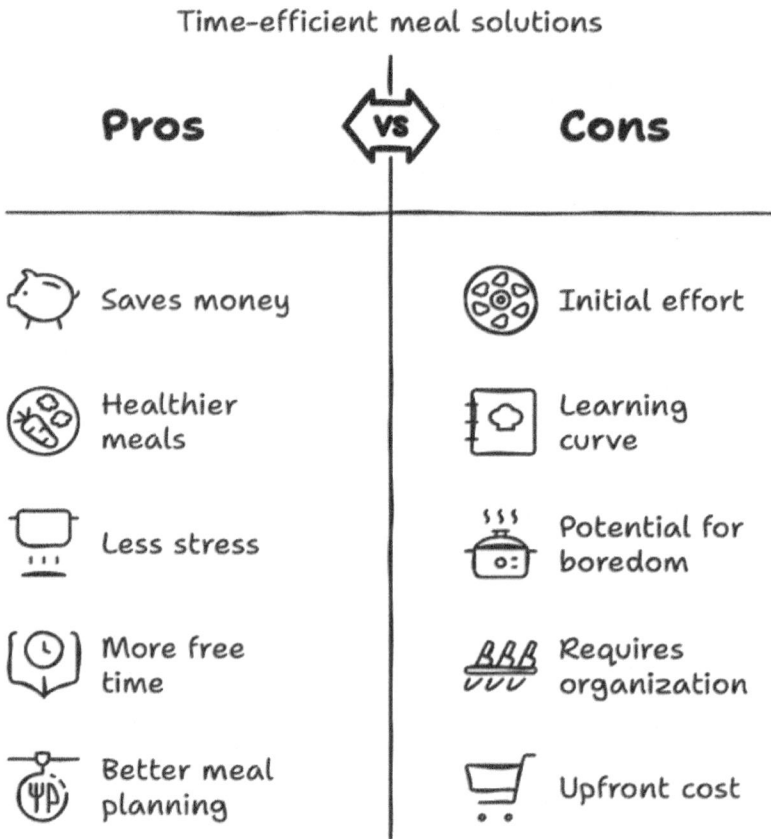

In this chapter, we'll explore how to transform your kitchen into an efficient workspace where quick, budget-friendly meals become second nature. You'll discover how simple changes to your kitchen layout, strategic prep work, and innovative tool usage can dramatically reduce cooking time and food costs. Whether cooking for one or feeding a family, these time-saving techniques will help you break free from the expensive cycle of convenience foods and takeout.

During my busiest season at work, I spent nearly $400 a month on takeout simply because I felt too exhausted to cook. One particularly stressful Wednesday, after ordering delivery for the third time that week, I decided to time myself making a simple stir-fry from scratch. To my surprise, it took only 12 minutes longer than waiting for delivery – and cost a fraction of the price. This revelation led me to experiment with kitchen efficiency, timing my meal prep tasks and reorganizing my kitchen workflow. I created a 'quick-prep station' near my stove with frequently used ingredients and tools, started pre-chopping vegetables on weekends, and learned to use my pressure cooker for lightning-fast meals. In just a month, I was able to reduce my food expenses by half, all while spending less time in the kitchen compared to relying on takeout. This experience taught me that with the right setup and strategies, preparing quick meals and cooking on a budget can not only coexist but also enhance each other.

The methods and strategies we'll explore in this chapter aren't just about cooking faster – they're about cooking smarter. You'll learn how to set up your kitchen for maximum efficiency, master time-saving preparation techniques, and discover the joy of creating delicious, nutritious meals in less time than you might spend scrolling through delivery apps. By the end of this chapter, you'll have a practical toolkit for transforming your kitchen routine from a time-consuming chore into an efficient, money-saving operation.

Perhaps most importantly, you'll discover that eating well on a budget doesn't require hours in the kitchen. You can prepare healthy, satisfying meals that respect your time and wallet with the right approach. Let's begin by examining how to set up your kitchen for success, creating an environment where quick, budget-friendly cooking is possible and enjoyable.

Strategic Preparation: Setting Up for Speed and Success

The foundation of quick, budget-friendly cooking lies in strategic kitchen preparation. When I began my efficiency journey, I spent an entire week-end analyzing my kitchen workflow, timing my movements, and noting how many extra steps I took to gather essential ingredients. What I discovered was eye-opening – I was wasting precious minutes simply because my kitchen wasn't organized for efficiency.

Strategic Kitchen Preparation for Efficiency

Analyze Kitchen Workflow	Identify Inefficiencies	Establish Prep Zone	Create Cooking Zone	Set Up Storage Zone

The first step in creating a speed-friendly kitchen is establishing dedicated zones.

Think of your kitchen as a professional workspace, with each area serving a specific purpose.

Create a prep zone near your sink for washing and chopping vegetables, a cooking zone near your stove with frequently used oils and seasonings, and a storage zone for efficiently packing leftovers.

This simple organization can save countless steps and minutes during meal preparation.

One of my most effective discoveries was creating a 'quick-grab station.' This designated area, ideally near your primary cooking space, houses your most frequently used items. In my kitchen, this includes:

Frequently used items – quick grab
- Essential seasonings (**salt, pepper, garlic powder**)

- **Cooking oils and vinegars**

- Commonly used utensils (**wooden spoons, spatulas, tongs**)

- **Measuring cups and spoons**

- A **small cutting board** for quick tasks

The power of proper organization extends to your refrigerator and pantry as well. Arrange ingredients by frequency of use, keeping everyday items at eye level and within easy reach. Store similar items together – all canned goods in one area, grains and pasta in another, and baking supplies in their section. This speeds up cooking and helps prevent overbuying items you already have.

Another game-changing strategy is implementing a prep-ahead principle. This involves dedicating a small amount of time, usually on weekends, to prepare ingredients you'll use throughout the week.

Key prep-ahead tasks that save significant time include:
- Washing and chopping hardy vegetables

- Portioning proteins into meal-sized amounts

- Preparing homemade seasoning blends

- Cooking basic grains or legumes

The most crucial aspect of strategic preparation is maintaining an organized storage system. Clear containers allow you to quickly identify ingredients, while uniform shapes stack efficiently to maximize space. Label everything with contents and dates – this simple step prevents waste and helps maintain your budget by ensuring you use items before they spoil.

The final piece of the efficiency puzzle is creating a cleaning strategy that works alongside your cooking. Keep a bowl for food scraps on your counter while preparing meals, and clean as you go rather than leaving everything for the end. Position your trash and recycling bins where they're easily accessible during food prep, and keep cleaning supplies within reach but safely away from food preparation areas.

Remember, the goal isn't to create a picture-perfect kitchen that belongs in a magazine – it's to design a functional space that serves your needs efficiently. Start with these basic organizational principles, then adjust them based on your cooking style and kitchen layout. As you implement these changes, you'll find that cooking becomes faster and more enjoyable, making it easier to stick to your budget-friendly meal plans.

꙳꙳꙳꙳ ꙳꙳꙳꙳

One-Pan Wonders: Quick Cooking with Minimal Cleanup

My love affair with one-pan cooking began during a particularly hectic month when my dishwasher broke down. Faced with the prospect of hand-washing a sink full of pots and pans each night, I discovered that necessity truly is the mother of invention. What started as a temporary solution to minimize cleanup became a cornerstone of my budget-friendly cooking strategy, saving time, effort and money on my utility bills.

Elements of One-Pan Cooking Success

Time Management
Efficient scheduling to ensure meal readiness

Cooking Vessel
The essential tool for preparing meals in one pan

Cooking Techniques
Methods that optimize ingredient preparation

Flavorful Ingredients
Key components that enhance the dish's taste

One-pan cooking is exactly what it sounds like – preparing complete meals using a single cooking vessel. But don't let the simplicity fool you; these dishes can be just as flavorful and nutritious as meals requiring multiple pots and pans. The key lies in understanding how different ingredients cook and combining them to create layers of flavor while maintaining proper cooking times.

The beauty of one-pan cooking extends beyond just easier cleanup. By cooking ingredients together, you create natural flavor infusions that might otherwise require expensive specialty ingredients. When vegetables cook alongside proteins, they absorb the savory juices typically lost to multiple cooking vessels. This method also helps reduce energy usage, as you only heat one cooking surface instead of numerous burners or ovens.

When selecting your essential one-pan cooking vessel, consider investing in a quality piece that will last years.

My workhorse is a 12-inch stainless steel skillet with deep sides, but here are several options to consider based on your cooking style and budget:

- Large cast iron skillet (excellent heat retention, naturally non-stick when seasoned)

- Deep stainless steel sauté pan (versatile and durable)

- Sheet pan (perfect for roasting meals)

- Large non-stick skillet (ideal for beginners)

- Enameled cast iron braiser (great for both stovetop and oven use)

The key to successful one-pan cooking is understanding the sequence of adding ingredients. Start with items that take the longest to cook, then add quicker cooking ingredients in stages. This prevents overcooking while ensuring everything finishes at the same time. For example, when making a chicken and vegetable skillet dinner, you might start by browning the chicken, then add hardy vegetables like carrots, followed by quicker-cooking items like zucchini, and finally, tender greens that need just a minute or two to wilt.

One of my favorite budget-friendly one-pan techniques. This involves preparing a simple protein and vegetable base that can be transformed into meals throughout the week by changing the seasonings and additions.

For instance, a basic chicken and vegetable skillet can become Italian with herbs and tomatoes, Mexican with cumin and chili powder, or Asian-inspired with soy sauce and ginger.

Essential tips for one-pan success:
- Cut ingredients into uniform sizes for even cooking

- Don't overcrowd the pan – food should have room to brown, not steam

- Keep a splash of broth or water nearby to deglaze the pan and capture flavors

- Use herbs and spices generously to create depth of flavor

- Consider texture when planning your meal – combine crispy, tender, and soft elements

One-pan cooking also lends itself beautifully to budget-friendly ingredients. Often among the least expensive produce options, root vegetables work perfectly in these dishes. Tough cuts of meat become tender when simmered with vegetables and aromatics. Even humble ingredients like beans and rice can be transformed into satisfying one-pan meals with the right combination of seasonings and techniques.

The cleanup benefits of one-pan cooking extend beyond just having fewer dishes to wash. When you cook everything in one vessel, you're also saving on water and dish soap, making this method both environmentally and economically sustainable. To make cleanup even more manageable, consider lining sheet pans with parchment paper or foil when appropriate and deglazing your pan with liquid, while it's still hot to prevent stuck-on food from becoming difficult to remove.

As you experiment with one-pan cooking, remember that some of the best recipes come from creative necessity. Don't be afraid to adapt and experiment with different combinations of ingredients based on what's available and affordable. The goal is to create delicious, nutritious meals while keeping your kitchen and budget clean and organized.

Smart Appliance Strategies: Maximizing Your Kitchen Tools

When I first inherited my grandmother's pressure cooker, it sat untouched in my cabinet for months. Like many home cooks, I was intimidated by unfamiliar kitchen tools, worried about safety, and unsure if the learning curve would be worth the investment of time. That pressure cooker eventually became my secret weapon for budget-friendly cooking, but only after I learned to approach kitchen appliances with a strategic mindset.

Modern kitchen appliances can be powerful allies in your quest for budget-friendly cooking, but only if you use them effectively. The key isn't having every gadget on the market – it's about choosing and using tools that genuinely serve your cooking style and budget goals. In my kitchen, each appliance must earn its counter space by contributing to either time savings or cost reduction, preferably both.

Essential appliances that offer the biggest return on investment for budget cooking:

- Slow cooker or pressure cooker (transforms tough, inexpensive cuts of meat)

- Food processor (speeds up prep work and makes homemade versions of expensive prepared foods)

- Blender (perfect for soups, smoothies, and sauces)

- Rice cooker (ensures perfect grains while freeing you to prepare other dishes)

- Kitchen scale (helps with portion control and precise recipe scaling)

The secret to maximizing these tools lies in understanding their full potential. For instance, your food processor isn't just for chopping vegetables – it can knead the dough, make nut butter, grind meat, and create homemade versions of expensive store-bought items like hummus or pesto. My food processor paid for itself within two months through the savings on store-bought hummus and nut butters.

Temperature control is another crucial aspect of appliance efficiency. Using the correct heat settings improves your cooking results, saves energy, and prevents food waste. For example, when using a slow cooker, the low setting is often more energy-efficient and better for tenderizing tough cuts of meat than the high setting. Similarly, understanding your oven's hot spots and temperature variations can prevent burned or unevenly cooked food.

Storage and maintenance of your appliances are also vital to their longevity and effectiveness. Keep user manuals in a designated folder or digitally on your phone for quick reference. Create a simple cleaning schedule to ensure each appliance stays in top condition – a well-maintained appliance works more efficiently and lasts longer, protecting your investment.

Key strategies for maximizing your kitchen tools:

- Use appliance timers to avoid overcooking and wasted energy

- Batch process ingredients when using food processors or blenders

- Keep frequently used appliances easily accessible

- Store seasonal appliances in less accessible spaces

- Clean tools immediately after use to prevent buildup and damage

---

One of my favorite money-saving strategies is maximizing efficiency using multiple sequential tools. For example, I might use my food processor to chop vegetables for the week, then immediately use it to prepare a homemade sauce, followed by a quick clean and use for grinding nuts for homemade granola. This approach minimizes cleanup time and makes the most of the energy used.

Consider the actual cost of ownership when evaluating kitchen appliances. A quality appliance that lasts for years and serves multiple purposes is often more economical than several cheaper, single-purpose tools. When I replaced my bargain-store blender with a higher-quality model, I could make everything from smooth soups to nut butter, eliminating the need for several other gadgets.

Remember that even the most essential kitchen tools can be appropriately maximized. A sharp knife and cutting board might be more efficient than an expensive gadget. The key is understanding when to use each tool and how to get the most value from it. Start with mastering the tools you have before investing in new ones, and always consider how each appliance fits into your overall cooking strategy and budget goals.

Learning to use your kitchen tools effectively is an investment in your culinary future. Each time you master a new technique or discover a new use for an appliance, you're building skills that will save you money and time in the kitchen. The goal isn't to have every gadget available but to make the most of the tools you choose to keep in your kitchen arsenal.

15-Minute Meal Solutions: Quick and Budget-Friendly Recipes

The concept of 15-minute meals often seems too good to be true, but I discovered their reality during a particularly challenging month when working late became the norm rather than the exception. The secret lies not in rushing through cooking but strategic preparation and recipe selection. These quick meals have become the backbone of my budget-friendly kitchen, saving both time and money while delivering satisfying, nutritious results.

The key to successful 15-minute cooking is the 5-5-5 method.

15-Minute Cooking Method

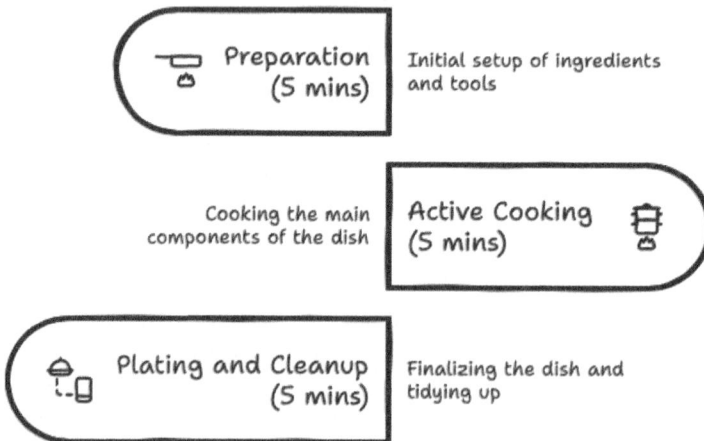

Preparation (5 mins) — Initial setup of ingredients and tools

Cooking the main components of the dish — Active Cooking (5 mins)

Plating and Cleanup (5 mins) — Finalizing the dish and tidying up

This approach ensures that a home-cooked meal remains within reach even on your busiest days. Let's explore some essential strategies and recipes that make this possible.

15-minute meal foundation with these essential pantry items:

- Quick-cooking proteins (canned beans, eggs, canned tuna)

- Instant grains (quick-cooking rice, couscous)

- Pre-washed greens

- Shelf-stable sauces and seasonings

- Frozen vegetables

These ingredients form the basis of countless quick meals, and buying them in bulk when on sale helps maintain your budget. I keep these items organized on a shelf dedicated to my pantry, where everything needed for quick meals is within arm's reach.

One of my go-to 15-minute solutions is a grain bowl formula. Start with a quick-cooking grain base, add a protein, pile on vegetables (raw or quickly sautéed), and finish with a flavorful sauce. For example, couscous (5 minutes to prepare) topped with canned chickpeas, cherry tomatoes, cucumber, and a quick tahini dressing creates a satisfying Mediterranean-inspired meal that costs roughly $2.50 per serving.

Here's a budget-friendly favorite that exemplifies the 5-5-5 method:

Quick Egg and Vegetable Stir-Fry
- Prep (5 minutes): Beat eggs, chop any fresh vegetables

- Cook (5 minutes): Scramble eggs, stir-fry fresh vegetables

- Finish (5 minutes): Combine all cooked ingredients with pre-cooked rice, add sauce, plate

The cost per serving typically runs under $2, making it an excellent option for budget-conscious cooks. The beauty of this template is its flexibility – you can use whatever vegetables are on sale or in season, and the protein can be easily swapped based on what's available and affordable.

Temperature management plays a crucial role in 15-minute cooking. Start with your highest-heat tasks, like boiling water or heating a pan, while preparing other ingredients. This parallel processing approach maximizes efficiency and ensures everything finishes at the right time.

Essential tips for successful 15-minute meals:

- Keep your most-used tools within easy reach

- Use pre-cut vegetables when they're on sale

- Master the art of parallel tasks

- Clean as you cook to minimize post-meal cleanup

- Keep a well-stocked 'speed shelf' of quick-cooking ingredients

---

One of my favorite time-saving techniques on weekends is to prepare versatile ingredients that can be quickly combined into different meals throughout the week. For instance, a batch of cooked quinoa can become a breakfast porridge, lunch grain bowl, or dinner side dish with just a few minutes of additional preparation.

Remember that 15-minute meals don't have to mean sacrificing nutrition or flavor. By keeping a variety of vegetables (both fresh and frozen), lean proteins, and whole grains on hand, you can create balanced meals that satisfy your schedule and budget. The key is planning ahead and keeping your kitchen organized for quick assembly.

For those with dietary restrictions, these quick meals can be easily adapted. Gluten-free grains like quinoa or rice can replace couscous, plant-based proteins can substitute for animal products, and most recipes can be modified to accommodate various allergies or preferences without significantly impacting preparation time or cost.

The beauty of mastering 15-minute meals lies in their ability to break the expensive cycle of takeout and convenience foods. When you know you can prepare a satisfying, nutritious meal in less time than it takes to wait for delivery, the temptation to order in naturally diminishes. This benefits your budget and gives you greater control over your nutrition and portion sizes.

As you build your repertoire of quick meals, keep a notebook of successful combinations and timing strategies. Note which ingredients work well together and which preparations yield the best results in minimal time. This personal reference will become invaluable as you develop your quick-cooking skills and adapt recipes to your taste and budget.

Prep-Ahead Techniques: Weekday Time-Saving Strategies

My journey into prep-ahead cooking began one Sunday evening when I realized I'd spent over $100 on takeout lunches the previous week simply because I hadn't planned. That night, I devoted two hours to experimenting with prep-ahead techniques, and by Friday, I had saved nearly $75 on lunch expenses alone. This experience taught me that strategic preparation isn't just about saving time – it's about protecting your budget while maintaining healthy eating habits.

The foundation of successful prep-ahead cooking lies in understanding the staying power of different ingredients. Through trial and error, I organize ingredients and tasks based on how well they hold up over time. Here's my tested preparation hierarchy:

Sunday Prep (keeps 5-7 days):
- Whole grains and legumes

- Roasted hardy vegetables (carrots, sweet potatoes)

- Homemade dressings and sauces

- Portioned proteins

Mid-Week Prep (keeps 2-3 days):
- Cut fresh vegetables

- Cooked pasta

- Prepared salad greens

- Mixed grain bowls

Day-Of Prep (best fresh):
- Avocados

- Seafood

- Delicate herbs

- Crispy toppings

One of the most valuable lessons I've learned is the importance of proper storage techniques. Investing in a set of quality glass containers wasn't just about organization – it dramatically extended the life of my prepped ingredients. I store cut vegetables with a paper towel to absorb excess moisture, keep herbs fresh in water like flowers, and use mason jars to maintain the crispness of prepared salads.

The key to successful prep-ahead cooking lies in batching cooking. Rather than preparing complete meals in advance, focus on versatile components that can be mixed and matched throughout the week. For instance, a single batch of roasted vegetables can serve multiple purposes: as a side dish, in grain bowls, blended into soups, or as a sandwich filling.

Efficient Sunday Prep for Weekday Success

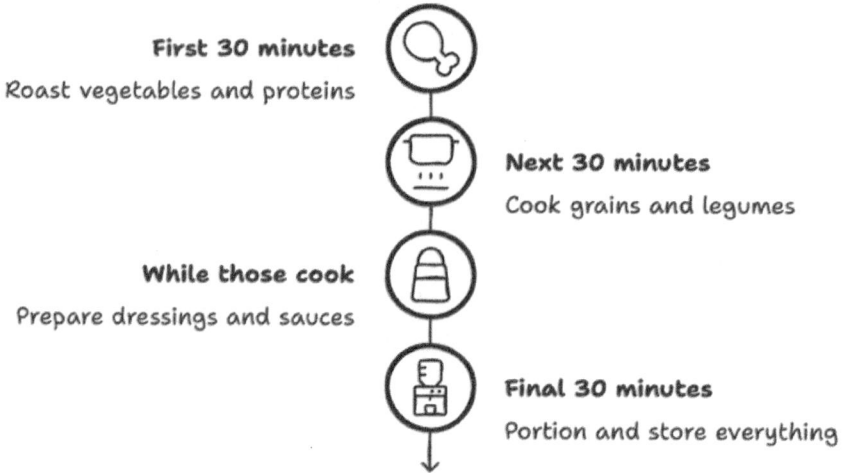

First 30 minutes
Roast vegetables and proteins

Next 30 minutes
Cook grains and legumes

While those cook
Prepare dressings and sauces

Final 30 minutes
Portion and store everything

Temperature management is crucial for food safety and quality. I always let ingredients cool completely before storing them, using a simple timer system to ensure nothing sits out too long. Hot foods go into shallow containers and are cooled on a rack before refrigeration, ensuring they reach a safe temperature quickly while maintaining their texture.

One of my favorite prep-ahead techniques involves preparing a few versatile base ingredients that can be transformed into different meals throughout the week. For example, a batch of quinoa might become:

- **Monday:** Mediterranean bowl with chickpeas and roasted vegetables

- **Tuesday:** Asian-inspired stir-fry with soy sauce and eggs

- **Wednesday:** Mexican-style burrito bowl with beans and salsa

The beauty of this approach lies in its flexibility and efficiency. By changing seasonings and add-ins, you prevent meal fatigue while maintaining the convenience of prep-ahead cooking. This method also helps manage your budget by allowing you to buy ingredients in bulk and use them across multiple meals.

Labeling is another crucial aspect of successful prep-ahead cooking. I use a simple system noting each container's preparation date and intended use-by date. This ensures food safety and helps prevent waste by clarifying what needs to be used first.

For those new to prep-ahead cooking, start small. Begin with just two or three components and gradually expand as you become comfortable with the process. Remember that the goal isn't to prepare everything in advance – it's to make your weekday cooking more efficient while maintaining quality and variety.

Perhaps most importantly, learn to adapt your prep-ahead routine to your schedule and eating habits. Some weeks allow for extensive preparation, while others permit basic tasks. The key is maintaining flexibility while prioritizing the preparations that have the most significant impact on your time and budget.

By incorporating these prep-ahead techniques into your weekly routine, you'll find that weekday meals become less stressful and more enjoyable. The initial time investment pays dividends in reduced food costs, less waste, and fewer last-minute takeout decisions. Remember, successful meal preparation isn't about perfection – it's about creating a sustainable system that works for your lifestyle and budget. As we conclude this chapter on quick-prep solutions and time-saving strategies, I'm reminded of my transformation from a takeout-dependent professional to an efficient home cook. The journey taught me that the key to successful budget cooking isn't just about speed – it's about creating systems that make healthy, affordable cooking the easiest choice.

Through the strategies we've explored – from setting up an efficient kitchen workspace to mastering one-pan cooking techniques – you now have the tools to break free from the expensive cycle of convenience foods and takeout. Remember that small changes, like organizing your 'quick-grab station' or implementing the 5-5-5 method for 15-minute meals, can significantly save time and money.

15-Minute Cooking Method

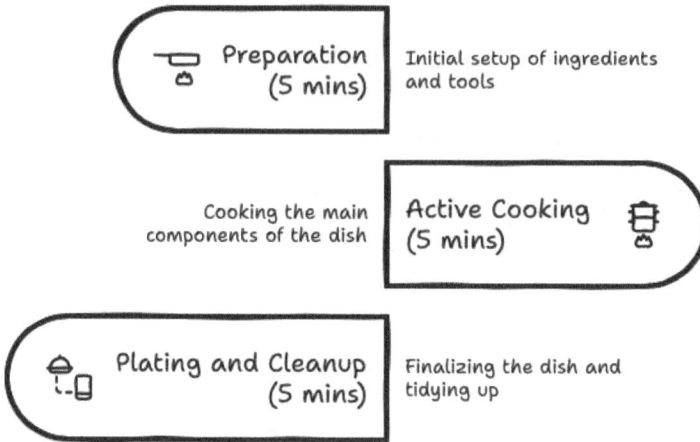

Preparation (5 mins) — Initial setup of ingredients and tools

Cooking the main components of the dish — Active Cooking (5 mins)

Plating and Cleanup (5 mins) — Finalizing the dish and tidying up

The prep-ahead techniques we've discussed aren't just about convenience; they're about creating a sustainable approach to cooking that respects both your schedule and your budget. By incorporating these strategies into your routine, you'll find that healthy, homemade meals become the natural choice, even on your busiest days.

Perhaps most importantly, we've learned that quick doesn't have to mean compromised. Whether you're preparing a simple stir-fry or assembling a grain bowl from prepped components, these efficient cooking methods can produce delicious, nutritious meals that cost a fraction of their takeout alternatives.

As you begin implementing these strategies in your own kitchen, remember that efficiency is a skill that develops with practice. Start with one or two techniques that resonate most with your lifestyle, and gradually incorporate others as you become more comfortable. The goal isn't perfection – it's progress toward a more organized, efficient, and budget-friendly approach to cooking.

With the foundation of quick-prep techniques now firmly established, you're ready to move forward with confidence, knowing that delicious, affordable meals are within reach, even on your busiest days. The time you invest in organizing your kitchen and mastering these strategies will pay dividends not just in your budget, but in your overall quality of life.

Remember, the most successful budget-conscious cooks aren't the ones who never face challenges – they're the ones who have systems in place to overcome them efficiently. By incorporating these time-saving strategies into your routine, you've taken a significant step toward sustainable, affordable, healthy eating habits that will serve you well for years to come.

Chapter Five

Frugal Family Favorites

Scaling Recipes for Any Household

Scaling recipes is like conducting an orchestra – each ingredient must be adjusted in perfect harmony to create a masterpiece that works for any size audience. When I first learned to adapt my grandmother's beloved lasagna recipe from feeding twelve to serving myself, I discovered that successful recipe scaling requires more than simple mathematics. As I found during my culinary journey, scaling recipes involves understanding the science and artistry of cooking. Each ingredient plays a vital role in the final dish, and adjusting quantities requires more finesse than simply dividing or multiplying numbers. The challenge lies in maintaining proper ratios and preserving the recipe's essence while adapting it to serve different household sizes.

Whether cooking for one or feeding a growing family, mastering the art of recipe scaling can transform your kitchen efficiency and budget management. I learned this lesson firsthand when I began hosting my neighborhood cooking workshops, where participants ranging from solo cooks to expanding families came together to learn these essential skills.

One memorable weekend, I decided to host a cooking workshop for my neighbors, focusing on scaling recipes for different household sizes. Among the participants was Mary, a recently widowed senior learning to cook for one, and the Albertsons, a young couple expecting triplets who needed to learn about scaling up. Using my signature chili recipe as an example, we created three different versions: a single serving, a couple's portion, and a family-sized batch. The real breakthrough came when Mary discovered she could make a single portion and freeze individual servings, while the Albertsons learned how to multiply ingredients without overwhelming their pantry space. What started as a simple workshop became a monthly gathering where we tackled different recipes and shared storage solutions. This experience taught me that recipe scaling isn't just about adjusting measurements – it's about building confidence in the kitchen and creating meals that work for every stage of life.

In this chapter, We'll explore the fundamental principles of recipe scaling, from basic mathematical conversions to practical storage solutions. You'll learn how to adjust cooking times, modify seasonings appropriately, and adapt your kitchen equipment to accommodate different portion sizes. Most importantly, you'll discover how to maintain the integrity of your favorite recipes while making them work for your specific household needs.

The beauty of mastering recipe scaling lies in its versatility. Whether you're downsizing a family recipe for solo dining or scaling up a favorite dish for meal prep, these skills will help you cook more efficiently while maintaining both flavor and budget consciousness. Let's dive into the techniques that will transform your cooking experience and empower you to create perfectly portioned meals for any situation.

Recipe Mathematics: Understanding Scaling Ratios and Conversions

Understanding recipe mathematics is essential for successful meal planning and budget management. When I first started scaling recipes, I
made the mistake of thinking I could divide or multiply every ingredient
equally. One memorable cooking disaster involved halving a cake recipe
where I reduced the leavening agents by exactly half, resulting in a dense,
unappetizing brick instead of the light, fluffy dessert I had envisioned.
This experience taught me that recipe scaling requires mathematical
precision and an understanding of how ingredients interact.

Let's start with the basics of recipe scaling. Most recipes can be adjusted
using a simple scaling factor.

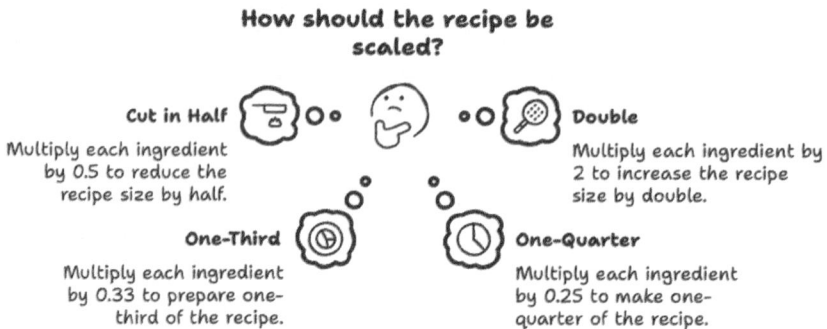

How should the recipe be scaled?

Cut in Half
Multiply each ingredient
by 0.5 to reduce the
recipe size by half.

Double
Multiply each ingredient by
2 to increase the recipe
size by double.

One-Third
Multiply each ingredient
by 0.33 to prepare one-
third of the recipe.

One-Quarter
Multiply each ingredient
by 0.25 to make one-
quarter of the recipe.

However, certain ingredients require special consideration when scaling.
Spices, herbs, and seasonings often don't follow strict mathematical
ratios. When reducing a recipe, you'll typically need to use slightly more
than the mathematical conversion suggests. Conversely, when increasing
a recipe, you'll need slightly less. I learned this principle while adapting
my favorite curry recipe – when I doubled the spices exactly, the dish
became overwhelmingly intense.

Liquid measurements require particular attention when scaling recipes. Here's a quick reference guide for common conversions.

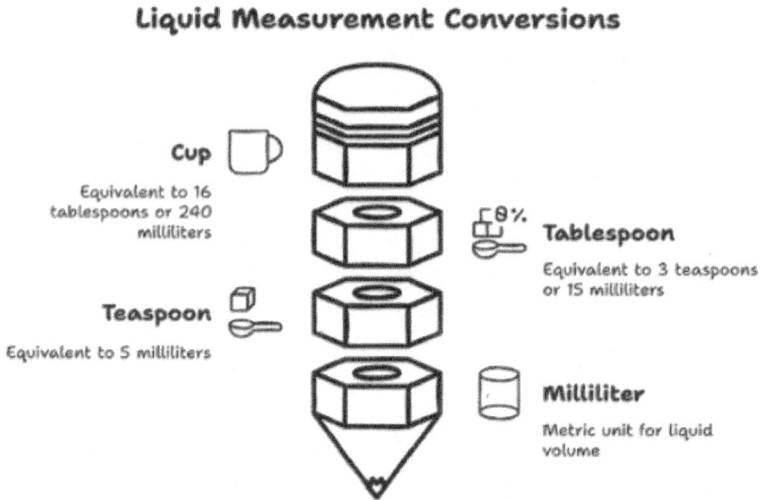

Liquid Measurement Conversions

Cup
Equivalent to 16 tablespoons or 240 milliliters

Tablespoon
Equivalent to 3 teaspoons or 15 milliliters

Teaspoon
Equivalent to 5 milliliters

Milliliter
Metric unit for liquid volume

Temperature and cooking times don't scale linearly with recipe size. When halving a recipe, you'll typically need to reduce cooking time by about 1/4, not 1/2. Similarly, when doubling a recipe, you may need to increase cooking time by only 50%, not 100%. Monitor your dish closely and use visual and textural cues rather than relying solely on scaled timing.

One of the most valuable lessons I've learned about recipe scaling is the importance of taking notes. I keep a small notebook in my kitchen to record successful (and unsuccessful) scaling attempts. This practice has helped me understand how different ingredients and recipes respond to scaling adjustments.

When working with small quantities, precision becomes increasingly important. I recommend investing in a set of measuring spoons that includes 1/8 teaspoon and 1/16 teaspoon measurements for accurately scaling down recipes. Using millilitres for liquid measurements in small quantities can often be more precise than traditional cup measurements.

Here's a practical tip I discovered through trial and error when scaling down recipes that call for eggs.

Egg Equivalents / Substitute

1 Large Whole Egg	1 Large Egg White	1 Large Egg Yolk
= 3 Tablespoons liquid (using egg substitute)	= 2 Tablespoons	= 1 Tablespoon

Remember that some ingredients don't need exact scaling. For instance, if a recipe calls for "a pinch of salt" or "salt to taste," use your judgment rather than trying to calculate precise measurements. The same applies to ingredients like bay leaves – you might use one bay leaf whether making a full recipe or half portion.

When scaling recipes up or down, always consider your equipment capacity. A scaled-up recipe might require a larger pot than you own, while one scaled-down might cook better in a smaller pan than specified. I learned this lesson the hard way when I attempted to double a soup recipe, only to find it bubbling over the edges of my largest pot.

Finally, don't forget to consider storage solutions when scaling recipes. If scaling down, ensure you have appropriate small containers for leftovers. When scaling up, verify that you have adequate freezer space or storage containers before beginning. This forethought will help prevent waste and maintain the quality of your prepared meals.

Ingredient Management: Smart Substitutions and Divisible Portions

Innovative ingredient management begins with understanding how to substitute and divide ingredients effectively. During my early days of budget cooking, I discovered that learning to make intelligent substitutions saved money and often led to exciting new flavor combinations. One particularly enlightening moment came when I ran out of fresh herbs for a recipe and learned that dried herbs could work just as well with the proper conversion ratios.

I've developed some essential substitution guidelines over years of kitchen experimentation.

Recipe Substitutions

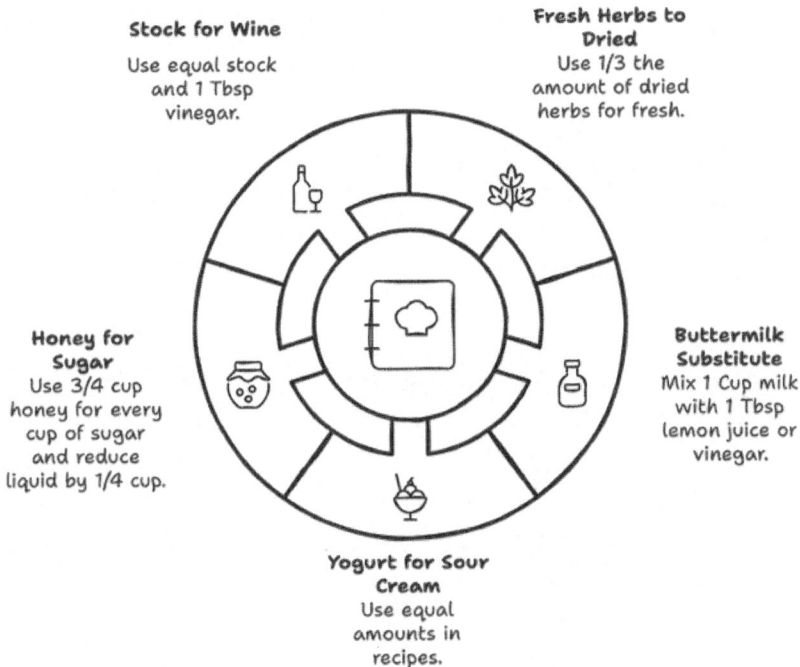

Stock for Wine
Use equal stock and 1 Tbsp vinegar.

Fresh Herbs to Dried
Use 1/3 the amount of dried herbs for fresh.

Honey for Sugar
Use 3/4 cup honey for every cup of sugar and reduce liquid by 1/4 cup.

Buttermilk Substitute
Mix 1 Cup milk with 1 Tbsp lemon juice or vinegar.

Yogurt for Sour Cream
Use equal amounts in recipes.

Managing portions effectively is crucial for both budget control and waste reduction. Many ingredients can be divided and stored for later use, maximizing their value across multiple meals. For example, when I buy a large package of chicken breasts, I immediately portion them into single servings before freezing. This makes defrosting easier and helps prevent waste from thawing too much.

One of the most valuable lessons about ingredient management is understanding shelf life and storage methods. Fresh herbs, for instance, can last much longer when appropriately treated. I keep tender herbs like cilantro and parsley upright in a glass of water with a loose plastic bag over the top, changing the water every few days. This method has extended their usable life from less than a week to nearly two weeks.

Divisible portions require strategic planning, especially when working with bulk ingredients. Here's my system for managing everyday bulk purchases:

- Large bags of rice: Divide into 2-cup portions in airtight containers

- Bulk meat packages: Separate into meal-sized portions before freezing

- Block cheese: Grate half and store in the freezer, keep half whole for slicing

- Fresh vegetables: Prep and portion for specific recipes within 2-3 days

When it comes to perishable ingredients, use it or lose it. This involves immediately processing ingredients that won't be used within their prime window. For example, if I notice bananas starting to over-ripen, I'll peel and freeze them for smoothies or future baking projects. This approach has dramatically reduced my food waste while ensuring I always have recipe-ready ingredients on hand.

Understanding ingredient density and concentration is crucial for successful substitutions. I discovered the truth through practice when substituting garlic powder for fresh garlic in my favorite pasta sauce. The result was overwhelmingly intense because I hadn't accounted for the concentrated nature of dried seasonings.

I follow this rule of thumb when substituting concentrated ingredients for fresh ones: start with one-quarter of the amount, then adjust to taste.

For those managing dietary restrictions, smart substitutions become even more critical.

Allergens have budget-friendly alternatives:
- All-purpose flour: Rice flour or oat flour (grind your own from whole oats)

- Eggs in baking: Mashed banana or applesauce (1/4 cup per egg)

- Dairy milk: Homemade oat milk (blend 1 cup oats with 4 cups water)

- Nuts: Roasted seeds (sunflower or pumpkin)

Perhaps the most valuable skill I've developed is learning to create "ingredient bridges" - using one ingredient across multiple recipes to minimize waste and maximize value. For example, when I buy a bunch of celery for soup, I plan several weekly recipes that use celery, ensuring the entire bunch gets used before it spoils. This approach requires considering your meal plan as an interconnected web rather than isolated recipes.

Remember that successful ingredient management isn't just about substitutions and divisions—it's about understanding how ingredients work together and maintaining quality while being resourceful. Mastering these principles will naturally create more efficient, cost-effective meals while reducing waste and maintaining flavor.

Equipment Adaptation: Right-Sizing Your Cooking Tools

When I started my budget cooking journey, my kitchen was cluttered with oversized pots and pans, impractical for single-portion cooking. One particularly frustrating evening, I attempted to make a small portion of rice in a large saucepan, which resulted in unevenly cooked grains and wasted energy. This experience taught me the importance of having appropriately sized cooking equipment for different portion sizes.

Right-sizing your cooking tools isn't about buying an entirely new kitchen set—it's about strategically selecting and using equipment that matches your cooking needs. I've found that a few well-chosen pieces can replace a cabinet full of rarely used items.

Essential tools for efficient small-batch cooking:
- 8-inch nonstick skillet for eggs and small sautés

- 2-quart saucepan for soups and grains

- Quarter-sheet pan for roasting vegetables

- 1.5-quart glass storage containers

- Collapsible measuring cups and spoons

One often-overlooked aspect of equipment adaptation is understanding how cooking times and temperatures change with different-sized tools. I've learned that a smaller pan often requires lower heat and shorter cooking times to prevent burning. This adjustment not only improves food quality but also saves energy.

The key to successful equipment adaptation is understanding the relationship between portion sizes and cooking vessel dimensions. Generally, ingredients should fill about two-thirds of any pot or pan for optimal heat distribution and cooking efficiency. This principle has helped me select the right tools for various recipes and avoid the common pitfall of using oversized equipment for small portions.

Maintaining appropriately sized equipment also contributes to better organization and workflow in the kitchen. I keep frequently used small tools in an easily accessible drawer near my prep area, while more significant, less-used items are stored in higher cabinets. This system has improved my cooking efficiency and made meal preparation more enjoyable.

Remember that adapting your kitchen equipment is an ongoing process. Start with the basics and gradually add or replace items as you discover your needs. Pay attention to which tools you use most frequently and which gather dust. This observation will guide you in creating a perfectly sized kitchen for your cooking style and household needs.

Storage Solutions: Preserving Scaled Portions Effectively

Proper storage is the cornerstone of successful recipe scaling and budget management. I learned by testing different approaches during my first attempt at batch cooking. I eagerly prepared multiple portions of my favorite curry only to discover that improper storage had led to freezer burn and wasted food. This experience taught me that preserving scaled portions effectively requires the right tools and proper techniques.

The foundation of practical storage begins with selecting the proper containers. Investing in high-quality, airtight containers in various sizes is essential for maintaining food quality. Here are the key features I look for in storage containers.

Features of Effective Storage Solutions

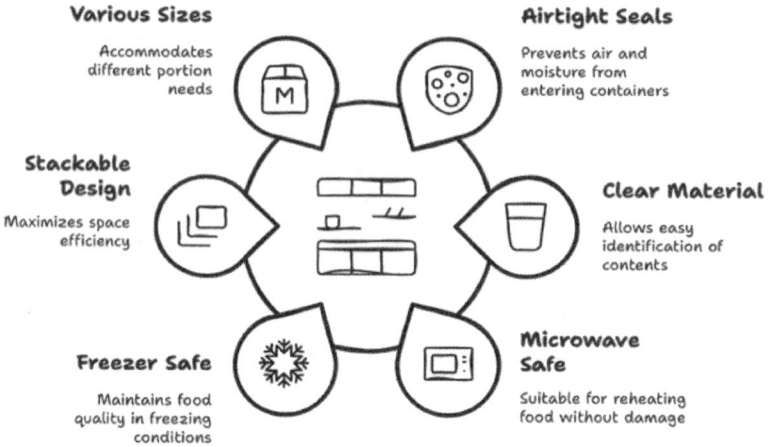

Various Sizes
Accommodates different portion needs

Airtight Seals
Prevents air and moisture from entering containers

Stackable Design
Maximizes space efficiency

Clear Material
Allows easy identification of contents

Freezer Safe
Maintains food quality in freezing conditions

Microwave Safe
Suitable for reheating food without damage

Proper preparation makes all the difference when it comes to freezer storage. Develop a method for first allowing food to cool completely to room temperature—this prevents condensation from forming inside containers, which can lead to ice crystals. Then, divide into appropriate portions based on your household size. Finally, store in containers with as little air space as possible to prevent freezer burn.

For refrigerated storage, organization is key to preventing waste. I arrange my refrigerator with these zones:

- Upper shelves: Ready-to-eat foods and leftovers

- Middle shelves: Dairy products and eggs

- Lower shelves: Raw meats and fish

- Crisper drawers: Fruits and vegetables

One of my most effective storage strategies is considering how I'll use the food in future meals. For example, when I make a large batch of tomato sauce, I freeze it in various portions—some in single-serving containers for quick pasta dinners, others in more significant portions for future casseroles.

Crucial labeling for effective storage management:
- Contents

- Date prepared

- Portion size

- Reheating instructions

- Use-by date

I use removable labels or erasable markers to make container reuse easier and more sustainable. This system has saved me countless times from the "mystery container" syndrome that often leads to food waste.

Understanding storage times is essential for maintaining food quality and safety. Here's my general guide for common scaled portions:

Effective Food Storage Guide

Cooked Vegetables

Preserved for 3-5 days refrigerated or 8-12 months frozen

Cooked Grains and Pasta

Stored for 3-5 days refrigerated or 6 months frozen

Cooked Meat and Poultry

Maintained for 3-4 days refrigerated or 2-6 months frozen

Soups and Stews

Kept for 3-4 days refrigerated or 4-6 months frozen

I've learned to scale recipes appropriately or plan for creative reuse for items that don't freeze well. Fresh herbs, for instance, can be preserved in oil and frozen in ice cube trays for future use. Leftover vegetables can be quickly pickled for extended storage.

Temperature control is crucial for food safety and quality maintenance. I keep a thermometer in my refrigerator and freezer to ensure they maintain proper temperatures.

Ensure proper food storage temperatures

Refrigerator
40°F (4°C) or
below

Freezer
0°F (-18°C) or
below

Remember to place newer items behind or below older ones to ensure first-in-first-out usage when storing multiple portions of the same dish. This simple practice has significantly reduced food waste in my kitchen.

Vertical storage solutions can maximize limited freezer and refrigerator space for those living in small spaces. I use stackable containers and organize items vertically rather than horizontally. This approach has doubled my storage capacity while keeping everything easily accessible.

Remember that different ingredients require different storage approaches. Sauces and soups can be frozen flat in freezer bags for space-efficient storage, while casseroles and baked goods often do better in rigid containers to maintain their structure.

By mastering these storage techniques, you'll be able to maintain the quality of your scaled portions while minimizing waste and maximizing your food budget. Proper storage isn't just about preserving food - it's about keeping your time and money invested in meal preparation.

Quality Control: Maintaining Flavor and Texture When Adjusting Portions

Maintaining consistent flavor and texture when scaling recipes is one of the most challenging aspects of portion adjustment. I discovered this truth during an ambitious attempt to quarter my mother's beloved meatloaf recipe. While the mathematics seemed straightforward, the final dish lacked the moisture and depth of flavor that made the original so special. This experience taught me that quality control requires more than precise measurements – it demands understanding how ingredients interact and contribute to the final result.

Certain ingredients significantly impact flavor and texture more than others when scaling portions up or down. Aromatics like onions, garlic, and herbs often need to be adjusted less dramatically than the main ingredients to maintain the intended flavor profile. For example, when halving a recipe, I typically reduce aromatics by only about 40% rather than 50% to ensure the dish remains well-seasoned.

Texture control requires particular attention when adjusting portions. Here are the key factors I consider for maintaining proper texture:

- Moisture content and distribution

- Protein structure and binding

- Starch development

- Cooking temperature and time

- Surface area to volume ratio

One of the most valuable lessons I've learned about quality control is the importance of understanding ingredient functions. Every ingredient serves a specific purpose: structure, moisture, flavor, or texture. When scaling portions, consider how each ingredient contributes to the final result.

Moisture management becomes particularly crucial when adjusting portions. Smaller portions tend to cook faster and can dry out more quickly, while more significant portions may need additional liquid to maintain proper consistency. Remember, for every 25% reduction in portion size, reduce cooking time by 15-20% and check moisture levels frequently during cooking.

Temperature control plays a vital role in maintaining quality across different portion sizes. Small portions often benefit from slightly lower cooking temperatures to prevent overcooking. More significant portions may need longer cooking times at consistent temperatures to ensure even heating.

Practical tips for maintaining quality when scaling portions:
- Use a food scale for precise measurements

- Adjust seasoning gradually, tasting as you go

- Monitor cooking temperatures with a reliable thermometer

- Keep detailed notes on successful adjustments

- Consider surface area when choosing cooking vessels

Binding agents and thickeners require special attention when scaling recipes. These ingredients often don't follow linear scaling rules. For example, when reducing a sauce recipe by half, you might need more than half the original amount of cornstarch to achieve the same thickness, as surface tension and evaporation rates change with volume.

The relationship between cooking time and portion size isn't always straightforward. I've learned to use visual and tactile cues rather than relying solely on scaled timing. For example, when scaling down a roasted vegetable recipe, I look for proper caramelization and tenderness rather than strictly following reduced cooking times.

Quality control also extends to ingredient preparation. Cutting vegetables and proteins into smaller pieces helps maintain proper cooking times and ensures even heat distribution when scaling down recipes. Conversely, keeping the original cut sizes but adjusting cooking times often yields better-scaling results.

Maintaining proper ratios becomes even more critical for baked goods. Leavening agents, in particular, require careful adjustment to ensure appropriate rise and texture. Scaling these recipes requires extra precision and often benefits from slight oven temperature and baking time adjustments to achieve the desired results.

Remember that successful quality control often requires some trial and error. Keep detailed notes about what works and what doesn't for different recipes and portion sizes. These records become invaluable references for future cooking projects and help develop an intuitive understanding of how various ingredients and techniques respond to scaling.

Finally, don't be afraid to adjust based on your observations and preferences. While maintaining the essence of a recipe is essential, scaling portions successfully often requires minor adaptations to achieve the best possible results. Trust your senses and experience as you develop strategies for maintaining quality across different portion sizes. As we conclude our exploration of scaling recipes for various household sizes, I'm reminded of that first cooking workshop where Mary and the Albertsons discovered the transformative power of proper portion adjustment. What began as a simple lesson in mathematics evolved into something far more meaningful – a journey of kitchen confidence and culinary independence.

This chapter covered the essential principles of recipe scaling, from understanding fundamental conversion ratios to mastering the nuances of ingredient adjustments. We've learned that successful scaling requires precision and intuition, whether dividing a family recipe into single servings or multiplying a favorite dish for batch cooking. The skills we've explored—from equipment adaptation to storage solutions—form a comprehensive toolkit for creating perfectly portioned meals that maintain quality and budget consciousness.

Perhaps most importantly, we've discovered that recipe scaling isn't just about numbers – it's about adapting our cooking approach to changing seasons. Whether you're cooking for one after years of family meals or expanding your recipe repertoire to feed a growing household, the principles we've discussed will help you maintain the integrity and enjoyment of your favorite dishes while meeting your current needs.

Remember that mastering portion control and scaling techniques is a journey, not a destination. Start with simple recipes, keep detailed notes of your successes and learning experiences, and don't be afraid to adjust based on your observations. With practice, you'll develop an intuitive understanding of how ingredients interact and how to maintain quality across different portion sizes.

As you progress with your cooking journey, I encourage you to experiment with our covered techniques. Try scaling your favorite recipes, test different storage methods, and adapt your kitchen equipment to suit your needs. Remember that every cook's journey is unique, and the skills you've learned here can be customized to fit your specific situation and preferences.

In the end, successful recipe scaling is about more than just serving sizes—it's about creating meals that nourish both body and soul, regardless of how many people gather at your table. Armed with these skills, you can handle any portion-sizing challenge while maintaining your budget and the joy of cooking.

Chapter Six

Love Your Leftovers

Creative Solutions for Zero Waste

Opening my refrigerator one Sunday evening, I faced the familiar sight of various containers filled with leftover ingredients from the week's meals, each representing both a challenge and an opportunity. That moment marked the beginning of my journey to master the art of creative leftover transformation, turning what many consider kitchen scraps into the foundation of delicious, budget-friendly meals. That simple moment became a turning point in my approach to cooking and food waste management, launching me into exploring creative ways to transform everyday leftovers into exciting new meals. In our modern world, where conscious consumption is more important than ever, learning to love your leftovers isn't just about saving money – it's about respecting our resources and reducing our environmental impact.

The journey to zero-waste cooking begins with the understanding that every ingredient has potential beyond its initial use. Those wilting herbs in your crisper drawer could become vibrant pesto, day-old bread can transform into crispy croutons, and yesterday's roasted vegetables might be tomorrow's gourmet quiche filling. By viewing our leftovers through this lens of possibility, we open ourselves to a world of culinary creativity while protecting our budgets.

During my early days of budget cooking, I faced what I now call 'The Great Rice Revolution.' After preparing too much rice for a stir-fry, I stared at three cups of leftover plain white rice in my refrigerator. Instead of letting it go to waste, I challenged myself to transform it over the next three days. I created a quick fried rice with frozen vegetables on the first day. On the second day, the remaining rice became creamy rice pudding for dessert. On the final day, I transformed the last portion into crispy rice cakes that became the base for a creative breakfast. This experience completely changed my perspective on leftovers. What started as a potential waste became an exercise in creativity that saved money and reduced food waste. Now, whenever I cook essential ingredients like rice, grains, or roasted vegetables, I intentionally make extra, knowing they'll become the building blocks for future meals. This approach has cut my food waste by over half and significantly reduced my grocery budget.

This chapter explores practical strategies for storing leftovers properly, creative techniques for transforming common ingredients, and innovative planning methods that help you cook once and eat twice – or thrice. You'll discover how to think like a chef when faced with leftover ingredients, learning to see possibilities where others might see waste. From proper storage techniques that extend freshness to clever recipe adaptations that breathe new life into yesterday's meals, you'll gain the confidence to tackle food waste head-on while keeping your meals interesting and your budget intact.

The techniques and strategies you'll learn here aren't just about being frugal – they're about being resourceful and mindful in your cooking journey. By mastering these skills, you'll save money and develop a more sustainable and creative approach to cooking that can transform your entire relationship with food. Let's begin exploring how to make the most of every ingredient in your kitchen, ensuring that nothing goes to waste while your meals remain delicious and satisfying.

Strategic Storage: Maximizing Leftover Shelf Life and Quality

Proper storage techniques are the foundation of successful leftover management. I learned this by making mistakes, such as losing an entire batch of homemade soup to spoilage simply because I'd stored it improperly. The correct container, temperature, and storage method can mean the difference between enjoying delicious leftovers and throwing away food and money.

Let's start with the essential rules of food storage that will help maximize the shelf life of your leftovers. Always cool food entirely before storing it, but don't leave it at room temperature for more than two hours. Use shallow containers for faster cooling and better storage – they allow food to reach safe temperatures more quickly and take up less space in your refrigerator. I keep a variety of clear, airtight containers in different sizes, which helps me choose the right size for leftovers and easily see what's inside.

Maximize Leftovers

- Use clear containers to identify contents easily

- Label everything with contents and date

- Store items at proper temperature zones in your refrigerator

- Keep raw and cooked foods separate

- Use airtight containers to prevent moisture loss and freezer burn

---

Temperature management is crucial for food safety and quality. Your refrigerator should be set at or below 40°F (4°C), while your freezer should maintain 0°F (-18°C) or lower. The door is the warmest part of your refrigerator, so reserve it for condiments and beverages rather than perishable leftovers. The bottom shelf, being the coldest, is ideal for storing meats and highly perishable items.

Creating a 'first in, first out' (FIFO) system in your refrigerator can help prevent food waste. Place newer leftovers behind older ones, ensuring older items get used first. I dedicate one shelf to leftovers and arrange items by date, making it easy to see what needs to be used soon. This simple organization method has dramatically reduced my food waste and helped me better use everything I cook.

Different types of leftovers require different storage approaches. Cooked grains and pasta should be stored in airtight containers for 3-5 days in the refrigerator. Leftover vegetables typically stay fresh for 3-4 days when properly stored, while cooked meats can last 3-4 days if refrigerated promptly. Most leftovers can be frozen for 2-6 months for extended storage, though quality may gradually decline.

Effective Food Storage Guide

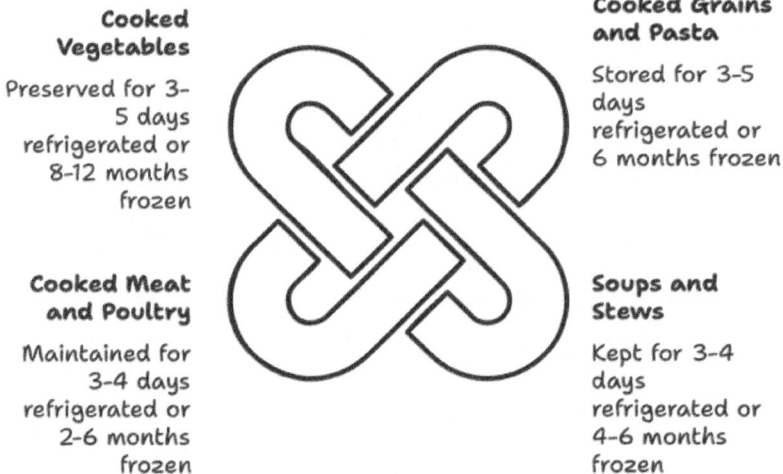

Cooked Vegetables

Preserved for 3–5 days refrigerated or 8-12 months frozen

Cooked Grains and Pasta

Stored for 3-5 days refrigerated or 6 months frozen

Cooked Meat and Poultry

Maintained for 3-4 days refrigerated or 2-6 months frozen

Soups and Stews

Kept for 3-4 days refrigerated or 4-6 months frozen

Proper packaging is essential when freezing leftovers to prevent freezer burn. Remove as much air as possible from storage containers or bags, and consider portioning foods into single servings for easier thawing. I like to use freezer-safe glass containers for soups and stews and heavy-duty freezer bags for items like cooked grains or shredded meats.

Always label frozen items with the contents and the date they were frozen.

One of my favorite storage tricks is creating a 'leftover inventory' sheet on my refrigerator. This simple list helps me track what needs to be used and when preventing forgotten containers from languishing in the back of the fridge. I update it whenever I add or use leftovers, making it easier to plan meals around what needs to be consumed first.

Proper storage is the first step in maximizing your leftovers' potential. Understanding how to store different foods correctly creates a foundation for transforming them into new, exciting meals. This knowledge helps prevent food waste and ensures that when you're ready to use your leftovers, they're still of the best quality and safe to eat.

⊱⊰

Ingredient Transformation: Creative Ways to Repurpose Common Leftovers

The art of transforming leftovers into entirely new dishes is like being a culinary alchemist – turning simple ingredients into gold. One of my favorite transformations began with a lonely roasted chicken carcass and some vegetable scraps that became the foundation for three distinct meals: a rich homemade stock, a hearty chicken and vegetable soup, and finally, a creamy chicken pot pie filling. This ingredient evolution stretches your food budget and adds variety to your weekly menu.

Let's explore fundamental techniques for transforming common leftovers into exciting new meals. The key is understanding the basic building blocks of cooking and how ingredients can play different roles in various dishes.

Leftover building blocks

- Cooked grains become stir-fries grain bowls or breakfast porridge

- Roasted vegetables transform into soups quiches or sandwich fillings

- Leftover meats can become salad toppings sandwich fillings or pasta additions

- Stale bread transforms into croutons breadcrumbs or French toast

- Wilting herbs become pestos herb oils or flavor boosters

One of my most successful transformation techniques involves a base recipe approach. This starts with preparing a versatile foundation that can evolve into multiple dishes throughout the week. For instance, a basic tomato sauce can become the base for pasta, pizza topping, shakshuka, or a flavorful soup. Similarly, roasted vegetables can transform from a simple side dish into a quiche filling, sandwich topping, or grain bowl base.

The secret to successful leftover transformation is understanding flavor profiles and texture combinations. When repurposing ingredients, consider how you can alter their texture or enhance their flavor to create something entirely new. For example, yesterday's plain rice can be crisped in a pan with eggs and vegetables for delicious fried rice or blended with milk and spices for creamy rice pudding.

- Transform plain proteins by shredding and adding new seasonings

- Revive tired vegetables by roasting or pureeing into soups

- Give new life to starches by crisping or incorporating them into new dishes

- Combine multiple leftovers into casseroles or one-pot meals

- Use aromatics and spices to create entirely new flavor profiles

One beneficial strategy I utilize is the planned leftover approach. Instead of waiting to see what remains after meals, I intentionally prepare extra portions of versatile ingredients that I know can be transformed. For instance, when roasting chicken, I'll prepare extra for salads, sandwiches, or enchiladas later in the week. This intentional approach to leftovers helps ensure I have the right ingredients for planned transformations.

Remember that texture is just as important as flavor when transforming leftovers. Soggy vegetables can be revived by roasting until crisp, tough meats can be shredded and incorporated into tacos or sandwiches, and soft grains can be formed into patties and pan-fried for a crispy exterior. These texture transformations can make leftover ingredients feel completely new and exciting.

When working with leftover proteins, consider changing their form and seasoning profile. Leftover roast chicken can be shredded and tossed with BBQ sauce for sandwiches, diced and seasoned with Mexican spices for tacos, or chopped and combined with curry paste for a quick Thai-inspired stir-fry. This approach helps prevent meal fatigue while making the most of your ingredients.

Remember the power of sauces and seasonings to transform leftovers completely. A simple vinaigrette can turn leftover roasted vegetables into a vibrant salad, while a spicy sauce can transform plain rice and beans into an exciting new meal. Keep a variety of basic sauces and seasonings on hand to help reinvent leftovers quickly and easily.

Planned Leftovers: Cooking Once, Eating Twice Strategy

The concept of planned leftovers revolutionized my approach to budget cooking. Rather than viewing leftovers as an afterthought, I began intentionally cooking more significant portions of versatile ingredients that could quickly transform into entirely different meals. This strategy saved money and significantly reduced my time in the kitchen while ensuring I always had interesting meals ready to go.

One of my most successful implementations of this strategy began with a Sunday roast chicken dinner. Instead of cooking just enough for one meal, I prepared a whole chicken with extra root vegetables. That initial meal provided a traditional roast dinner. Still, the remaining chicken and vegetables were strategically portioned for three additional meals: a quick chicken and vegetable soup, crispy chicken tacos with roasted vegetable salsa, and finally, a savory chicken and root vegetable pot pie. What started as one $12 chicken became four distinct meals, each with its unique flavor profile.

Strategic Meal Planning Overview

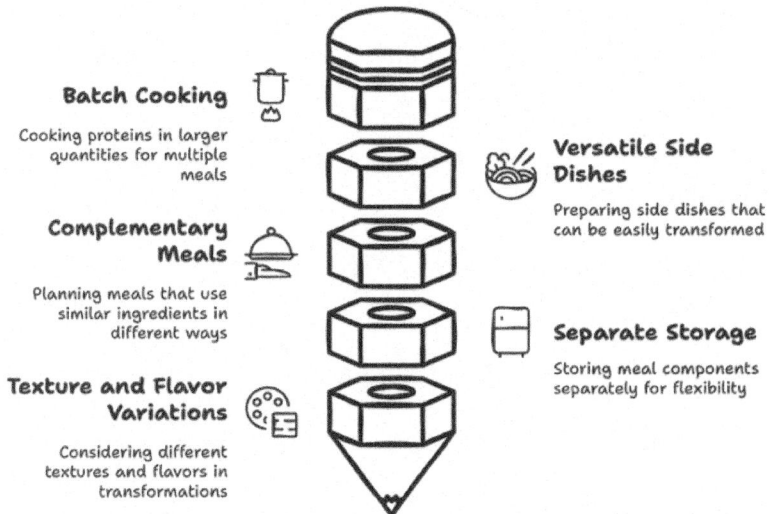

Batch Cooking

Cooking proteins in larger quantities for multiple meals

Versatile Side Dishes

Preparing side dishes that can be easily transformed

Complementary Meals

Planning meals that use similar ingredients in different ways

Separate Storage

Storing meal components separately for flexibility

Texture and Flavor Variations

Considering different textures and flavors in transformations

The key to successful planned leftovers lies in strategic preparation and storage. When cooking your initial meal, consider how each component might be repurposed. For example, when preparing rice, cook extra to use in stir-fries, rice pudding, or crispy rice cakes. When roasting vegetables, make additional portions that can be pureed into soup, added to sandwiches, or transformed into a hearty breakfast hash.

Temperature and timing play crucial roles in the planned leftover strategy. Always cool foods completely before storing them, and portion them according to your planned future uses. It is helpful to divide leftovers into meal-sized portions immediately after cooking, which prevents over-portioning and makes future meal prep more efficient.

One of my favorite planned leftover techniques involves component cooking. Instead of preparing complete dishes, I cook essential ingredients that can be mixed and matched throughout the week. For instance, I might roast a large batch of seasonal vegetables, prepare a pot of quinoa, and cook some chicken breasts. These components can be combined in different ways: Mediterranean-style grain bowls one day, Asian-inspired stir-fry the next, and wrapped in tortillas for quick burritos later in the week.

Mix and match basic ingredients
- Roasted vegetables become salad toppings, soup bases, or sandwich fillings

- Cooked grains transform into stir-fries, breakfast bowls, or side dishes

- Proteins can be shredded, diced, or sliced for various applications

- Basic sauces adapt to different cuisine styles

- Fresh herbs and spices create distinct flavor profiles

Proper storage and organization also depend on the success of planned leftovers. I maintain a simple spreadsheet that tracks my prepared components and suggests potential meal combinations. This system helps prevent food waste and ensures I use everything while it's still at its peak quality.

Remember that planned leftovers differ from regular leftovers because they're intentionally created with specific future meals in mind. This intentional approach helps avoid the monotony that sometimes comes with eating the same meal multiple times. Instead, each transformation feels like a fresh, new dish while capitalizing on the efficiency of cooking once and eating twice.

Start with one or two weekly components when implementing a planned leftover strategy. As you become more comfortable with the process, you can expand to preparing multiple components and planning more complex transformations. The goal is to balance efficiency and variety that works for your schedule and preferences.

❧❧❧❧ ❦❦❦❦

Zero-Waste Cooking: Using Every Part of Your Ingredients

My journey into zero-waste cooking began with carrot tops, which I was about to toss in the trash. Staring at the vibrant greens, I remembered my grandmother's wisdom about using every part of our ingredients. That moment sparked a revelation that transformed my approach to cooking – what we often consider 'scraps' can become the foundation for delicious, nutritious meals while stretching our food budget further.

Zero-waste cooking isn't just about being frugal; it's about respecting our ingredients and maximizing their potential. Every vegetable trim, herb stems, and meat bone can contribute to creating flavorful dishes while reducing our environmental impact. Let's explore how to make the most of common ingredients that often end up in the compost bin.

Flavorful ingredient rescue
- Vegetable peels and ends become rich stocks and broths

- Herb stems add flavor to soups and sauces

- Citrus zest and peels transform into flavor enhancers

- Stale bread becomes breadcrumbs or croutons

- Cheese rinds add depth to soups and stews

One of my favorite zero-waste techniques involves creating a stock bag in the freezer. Throughout the week, I collect vegetable trimmings – onion ends, carrot peels, celery leaves, mushroom stems – in a freezer bag. When the bag is full, these scraps become the base for a flavorful homemade stock that costs nothing but adds incredible depth to soups, risottos, and sauces.

Leafy greens often provide double duty in the kitchen. Beet tops can become sautéed side dishes or additions to salads, while radish greens make peppery pestos. Even broccoli stems, often discarded, can be peeled and sliced into delicate medallions for stir-fries or grated into slaws.

Meat and fish scraps deserve special attention in zero-waste cooking. Bones and shells make rich stocks, while fat trimmings can be rendered for cooking oil. Fish skin can be crisped up for a crunchy garnish or added to stocks for extra flavor.

Other zero waste ideas
- Use bones and shells for rich stocks

- Render fat trimmings for cooking

- Save pan drippings for gravies and sauces

- Freeze excess herbs in oil for future use

- Preserve citrus peels for zest and flavoring

Proper storage and organization are key to successful zero-waste cooking. Keep a designated container in your freezer for stock ingredients, and store vegetable trimmings in airtight containers until you're ready to use them. Label everything clearly with dates to ensure you use items while they're still at their best.

One particularly satisfying zero-waste technique involves using every part of fresh herbs. The leaves go into dishes as usual, while the stems can infuse oils, vinegars, or stocks. Woody herb stems like rosemary can be used as aromatic skewers for grilled vegetables or meats.

Remember that zero-waste cooking requires thinking ahead. When planning meals, consider how each ingredient can be used completely. For example, when buying a whole chicken, use the meat for several meals, the bones for stock, and even the rendered fat for future cooking. This approach reduces waste and maximizes the value of your grocery budget.

Remember the power of preservation in zero-waste cooking. Citrus peels can be candied or dried for future use, herb stems can be dried for tea, and vegetable scraps can be fermented into kimchi or pickles. These preservation techniques prevent waste and add variety to your pantry.

By embracing zero-waste cooking principles, you'll discover that what once seemed like kitchen scraps can become the secret ingredients that elevate your cooking while reducing your grocery bills. The satisfaction of using every part of your ingredients goes beyond saving money –

it connects us to a more sustainable and mindful way of cooking that honors both our resources and our environment.

⋙⟩⟩⟩ ⟨⟨⟨⋘

Safety First: Proper Storage and Reheating Guidelines

My most memorable lesson in food safety came from an incident I call 'The Potato Salad Predicament.' I had left a bowl of homemade potato salad out during a summer gathering, thinking a few hours at room temperature wouldn't hurt. Fortunately, a friend with food safety training noticed and explained the dangers of leaving perishable foods in the 'danger zone' – between 40°F and 140°F (4°C-60°C). That eye-opening experience taught me that proper food handling isn't just about preventing waste but protecting health and safety.

When it comes to storing and reheating leftovers, temperature control is your most important ally. Food should never sit at room temperature for over two hours or one hour if the ambient temperature is above 90°F (32°C). Bacteria multiply rapidly in the danger zone, potentially reaching harmful levels.

Proper cooling techniques are crucial for food safety:

- Cool foods quickly before refrigerating

- Store food at 40°F (4°C) or below

- Use shallow containers for faster cooling

- Divide large portions into smaller containers

- Label everything with contents and date

Large quantities of hot food should be divided into smaller portions and stored in shallow containers to cool quickly. I learned to use ice baths to rapidly cool soups and stews – place your container in a larger bowl filled with ice water and stir occasionally until cooled.

Temperature is equally important when it comes to reheating. All leftovers should be reheated to at least 165°F (74°C) to kill any bacteria that may have developed during storage. Use a food thermometer to verify the temperature, especially for dense foods like casseroles or thick soups.

Different foods require different reheating methods for the best results. While microwaving might work well for some items, others benefit from gentle stovetop heating or oven warming. Here are some general guidelines:

General reheating guidelines
- Soups and sauces: Reheat on the stovetop, stirring frequently

- Casseroles and pasta dishes: Cover and heat in the oven

- Rice and grains: Add a splash of water before reheating

- Vegetables: Steam or microwave briefly to prevent overcooking

- Meats: Heat slowly to avoid drying out

Storage duration is another critical factor in food safety. While properly stored leftovers can last several days, knowing the limits is essential. I keep a simple chart on my refrigerator as a quick reference.

Food Storage Duration Overview

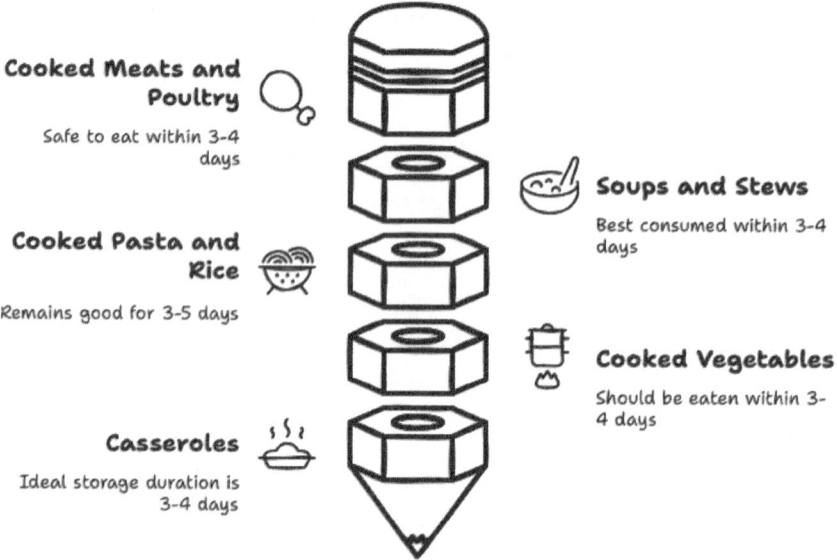

Cooked Meats and Poultry

Safe to eat within 3-4 days

Soups and Stews

Best consumed within 3-4 days

Cooked Pasta and Rice

Remains good for 3-5 days

Cooked Vegetables

Should be eaten within 3-4 days

Casseroles

Ideal storage duration is 3-4 days

When in doubt about a food's safety, remember the old adage: 'When in doubt, throw it out.' It's better to waste a small amount of food than risk foodborne illness. Look for signs of spoilage, such as unusual odours, mould growth, or changes in texture and colour.

Freezing is an excellent option for extending the life of leftovers beyond a few days. If properly packaged, most cooked foods can be frozen for 2-6 months without significant quality loss. Use freezer-safe containers or heavy-duty freezer bags, removing as much air as possible to prevent freezer burn.

When thawing frozen leftovers, always use the refrigerator method rather than leaving food at room temperature. While it takes longer – typically 24 hours for every 4-5 pounds – it's the safest approach. Never thaw food on the counter, as this can allow bacteria to multiply rapidly in outer portions while the center remains frozen.

Remember that not all containers are created equal regarding food storage. Use food-grade storage containers appropriate for your intended use—some are suitable for refrigeration but not for freezing or reheating. Glass containers with tight-fitting lids are my favorite as they're versatile, don't retain odors, and are easy to clean thoroughly.

Following these safety guidelines ensures that your budget-conscious approach to cooking and leftover management doesn't compromise food safety. Proper storage and reheating protects your health and helps maintain the quality and flavor of your carefully prepared meals. As we conclude our exploration of loving our leftovers, I'm reminded of how far my journey has come from those early days of staring at containers of leftover rice, wondering what to do next. The transformation from viewing leftovers as a challenge to seeing them as an opportunity has been revolutionary for my budget and my approach to cooking.

Throughout this chapter, we've discovered that managing leftovers is about more than just reheating yesterday's meals – it's about creative transformation, proper storage, and thoughtful planning. We've learned essential techniques for storing food safely, innovative methods for transforming ingredients, and strategies for intentionally planning meals that make the most of every ingredient.

The zero-waste cooking techniques we've explored help reduce food waste and maximize your grocery budget. From creating flavorful stocks from vegetable scraps to transforming stale bread into gourmet croutons, these methods show us that what might seem like kitchen waste can become the foundation for delicious new meals.

Most importantly, we've seen how proper food safety practices form the backbone of successful leftover management. Understanding temperature controls, storage duration guidelines, and proper reheating techniques ensures that your budget-conscious cooking approach never compromises safety.

As you implement these strategies in your kitchen, remember that mastering leftover management is a journey. As your confidence grows, you can expand your repertoire of transformation techniques and experiment with more complex preparations.

The skills you've gained in this chapter extend far beyond simple food storage. They represent a fundamental shift in how we think about food waste, budget management, and creative cooking. By embracing these principles, you're not just saving money; you're joining a growing movement of conscious cooks who understand that respecting our food resources is economically and environmentally responsible.

In our next chapter, we'll explore how to maintain these budget-conscious practices while accommodating special dietary needs. But for now, I encourage you to start your leftover transformation journey. Begin with a straightforward change – perhaps creating that freezer stock bag or planning your first intentional leftover meal. Remember, every small step toward reducing food waste and maximizing ingredients is a step toward financial savings and more sustainable cooking practices.

Your kitchen is now equipped with the knowledge to turn common leftovers into culinary gold, proving that with creativity and proper planning, yesterday's meals can become tomorrow's culinary adventures. The journey to zero-waste cooking starts with a single saved scrap—where will you begin?

Chapter Seven

Special Diets, Savvy Budget

Accommodating Restrictions Without Breaking the Bank

When I discovered my gluten intolerance during the height of my budget-conscious journey, I feared my carefully crafted meal-planning system would crumble under the weight of expensive specialty products. That fear transformed into determination as I learned to navigate the world of dietary restrictions while keeping my food budget intact, discovering that with the right strategies, special diets don't have to mean special prices. Like many people navigating dietary restrictions, I initially felt overwhelmed by the seemingly endless list of ingredients I needed to avoid and the premium prices of specialty products. However, through careful research and experimentation, I discovered that maintaining a special diet doesn't have to drain your bank account – it just requires a strategic approach to shopping, cooking, and meal planning.

Whether you're dealing with food allergies, celiac disease, or choosing a specific dietary lifestyle like vegetarianism or veganism, the key to budget-friendly special diets lies in focusing on naturally compliant whole foods rather than processed alternatives. By mastering simple substitutions and understanding which specialty items are worth the investment, you can create delicious, satisfying meals that meet your dietary needs without breaking the bank.

During my first month of adapting to a gluten-free diet, I faced the need to purge and rebuild the pantry. Standing in my kitchen, surrounded by ingredients I could no longer use, I calculated that replacing everything with gluten-free alternatives would cost nearly triple my monthly food budget. Instead of giving in to expensive pre-made products, I began experimenting with naturally gluten-free whole foods. When bought in bulk from international markets, I discovered that rice flour costs a fraction of branded gluten-free flour. I learned to make my oat flour from certified gluten-free oats, saving over 60% compared to pre-ground versions. Through careful research and experimentation, I transformed my kitchen into a safe, affordable space for my new dietary needs. Within three months, I had developed a system that kept my food costs only 15% higher than my previous budget while fully accommodating my dietary restrictions. This experience taught me that dietary restrictions don't have to break the bank – they require a different approach to shopping, cooking, and meal planning.

This chapter will explore practical strategies for maintaining a budget-friendly kitchen while accommodating various dietary restrictions. From sourcing affordable alternatives to adapting recipes and preventing cross-contamination, you'll discover how to create delicious, compliant meals without sacrificing your financial goals. Whether you're cooking for yourself or a family with multiple dietary needs, these techniques will help you navigate the challenges of special diets while keeping your food budget in check.

Remember, the goal isn't just to survive with dietary restrictions – it's to thrive while enjoying delicious, nutritious meals that respect your health needs and budget. With the right approach, you can transform what might seem like limiting dietary requirements into an opportunity to explore new ingredients, cooking techniques, and flavors that enhance your culinary journey.

Budget-Friendly Alternative Ingredients: Smart Substitutions for Common Allergens

One of the biggest challenges when dealing with food allergies or dietary restrictions is finding affordable substitutes for common ingredients. Through my experience and countless hours of kitchen experimentation, I've discovered that many everyday ingredients can be budget-friendly alternatives to expensive specialty products. Let's explore some smart substitutions that won't strain your wallet.

Regarding dairy alternatives, commercial options can quickly consume your grocery budget. Instead of relying on store-bought plant-based milk, I've found that making your oat milk costs mere pennies per serving. Blend one cup of rolled oats with four cups of water, strain through a fine-mesh cloth, and you'll have fresh oat milk at a fraction of the retail price. For baking, applesauce or mashed bananas can often replace eggs at about one-third the cost while adding natural sweetness to your recipes.

Gluten-Free Flour Alternatives

- Rice flour from Asian markets (often 70% cheaper than specialty stores)

- Ground oats (certified gluten-free if needed)

- Chickpea flour for protein-rich options

- Cornmeal for breading and cornbread

When I first started exploring nut-free options, I discovered sunflower seed butter could replace pricey almond butter in most recipes. Made from roasted sunflower seeds, it provides similar nutrition at about half the cost. For those avoiding soy, coconut aminos can substitute soy sauce. Still, a simple mixture of salt, mushroom powder, and a touch of molasses creates a surprisingly effective and much more affordable alternative.

Dairy Alternatives
- Coconut Milk is a versatile dairy substitute for cooking

- Nutritional Yeast adds a cheesy flavor to dishes

- Homemade Oat Milk is perfect for drinking and cereals

- Mashed Avocado provides a creamy texture in recipes

Protein substitutions often present a significant challenge, especially for those following plant-based diets. Rather than relying on expensive meat alternatives, I've learned to embrace legumes as my primary protein source. Lentils, particularly red lentils, can be transformed into convincing meat alternatives in dishes like tacos and pasta sauces while providing excellent nutrition at roughly one-fifth the cost of commercial meat substitutes.

One of my favorite money-saving discoveries has been the versatility of aquafaba – the liquid from canned chickpeas. This often-discarded ingredient can replace eggs in everything from meringues to mayonnaise, giving you a free egg substitute every time you use chickpeas. I keep a jar in my freezer, portioned into ice cube trays, ready to use in baking or as a recipe binder.

Egg Alternatives
- Ground flaxseed mixed with water

- Mashed banana for sweet recipes

- Aquafaba for baking and binding

- Chia seeds soaked in water

Arrowroot powder can seem expensive at first glance for those avoiding corn-based thickeners. However, I've found that international markets' potato starch or tapioca flour provides the same thickening power at a significantly lower price point. These alternatives work beautifully in gravies, sauces, and pie fillings.

Remember that successful substitution often requires some experimentation. I keep a small notebook in my kitchen documenting what works and what doesn't, including specific measurements and cooking time adjustments. This practice has saved me countless dollars in failed experiments and helped me develop a reliable collection of affordable alternatives that work consistently.

I've learned to look beyond the specialty food aisle when shopping for alternative ingredients. Many international markets carry naturally allergy-friendly ingredients at a fraction of the cost in conventional grocery stores. For example, rice flour, tapioca starch, and coconut milk are often significantly cheaper in Asian markets, while Middle Eastern stores typically offer better prices on seeds, nuts, and alternative grains.

The key to making alternative ingredients budget-friendly is to focus on versatility. I prioritize purchasing ingredients that can serve multiple purposes in my kitchen. For instance, chickpea flour can be used for flatbreads, as a binder in veggie burgers, and to thicken sauces, making it a worthwhile investment even at a slightly higher price point.

⟡

Strategic Shopping for Special Diets: Finding Affordable Specialty Products

Shopping for specialty diet products can feel like navigating a maze of premium prices and limited options. However, my experience has taught me that with strategic planning and insider knowledge, you can find affordable alternatives that meet your dietary needs without emptying your wallet. The key lies in knowing where, when, and how to maximize every dollar spent on specialty items.

One of my most valuable discoveries was that many specialty products are significantly cheaper at certain stores during specific times. I developed a rotating schedule, visiting stores monthly to maximize their best deals. For instance, I learned that my local natural foods store marks down gluten-free products on the first Tuesday of each month, while the larger chain supermarket offers the best deals on dairy alternatives during their mid-month sales.

During my budget-conscious journey, I discovered that many conventional grocery stores now carry store-brand versions of popular specialty products at significantly lower prices. These alternatives often match the quality of name-brand items while costing 30-40% less. I make a point to try store-brand versions of my most-used items, keeping a small notebook to track which ones meet my standards for both taste and texture.

Timing can make a significant difference in your specialty shopping success. Shopping early in the day often gives me first access to marked-down items, particularly in the fresh produce section, where I can find affordable organic options. Additionally, many stores reduce prices on specialty items approaching their 'best by' dates, offering an excellent opportunity to stock up on shelf-stable products.

Money-Saving Shopping Strategies

- Compare unit prices across different package sizes

- Check clearance sections for specialty items

- Sign up for store loyalty programs

- Use store apps for digital coupons

- Buy shelf-stable items in bulk when on sale

One of my most effective strategies has been building relationships with store managers and staff. By politely asking questions about their ordering cycles and markdown schedules, I've gained valuable insights into when specialty items are most likely to be discounted. This information has helped me plan my shopping trips more effectively and save significantly on my most-used items.

Regarding specialty produce, I've learned to embrace seasonal shopping. Instead of paying premium prices for out-of-season organic produce, I stock up when items are abundant and preserve them through freezing or dehydrating. This approach has allowed me to maintain a varied diet while managing costs.

Don't overlook the power of price matching and rain checks for specialty items. Many stores will 'match competitors' prices on identical items, including specialty products. I keep a small file of current ads on my phone and have saved considerable amounts by price matching, especially on more expensive specialty items like alternative flours and dairy-free cheese alternatives.

Storage Solutions for Bulk Purchases
- Airtight containers for flours and grains

- Vacuum-sealed bags for nuts and seeds

- Glass jars for homemade alternatives

- Freezer containers for bulk perishables

- Labeled storage with purchase dates

Remember that not every specialty item needs to come from the specialty aisle. Many regular grocery items naturally fit various dietary restrictions and often cost less than their 'specialty' counterparts. For instance, many ordinary corn tortillas are naturally gluten-free, and plain rice cakes can be found in regular aisles at lower prices than their specialty-labeled counterparts.

I've also found success in joining local buying clubs or co-ops focusing on specialty dietary needs. These groups often pool resources to purchase items in bulk directly from suppliers, resulting in significant savings. While the upfront cost is higher, the per-unit price makes it worthwhile for frequently used items.

Perhaps most importantly, I've learned to be flexible with my shopping strategy. Market conditions, product availability, and prices can change rapidly, so maintaining adaptability in your shopping approach is crucial. Keep a price book to track the best deals, and be willing to adjust your shopping routine as needed to maximize your savings on specialty items.

Cross-Contamination Prevention on a Budget: Safe Kitchen Setup Solutions

When I first started managing my gluten intolerance, I quickly realized that preventing cross-contamination didn't require expensive specialty equipment or a complete kitchen overhaul. Instead, it demanded thoughtful organization and creative problem-solving. I created a safe cooking environment through careful planning and strategic purchases while staying within my budget constraints.

The foundation of cross-contamination prevention starts with clever storage solutions. Rather than investing in expensive specialty containers, I repurposed clear plastic bins from the dollar store to create dedicated zones in my pantry and refrigerator. Using colourful washi tape and permanent markers, I developed a simple colour-coding system: red for allergen-containing items, green for safe foods, and yellow for items requiring careful handling.

Essential Budget-Friendly Storage Solutions
- Clear plastic bins for ingredient separation

- Masking tape and markers for labeling

- Reusable silicone bags for portioning

- Dollar store cutting boards in different colors

- Basic cleaning supplies for surface sanitization

One of my most effective money-saving strategies was creating designated preparation zones instead of duplicating every kitchen tool. I designated one corner of my counter as my 'safe zone,' using a large plastic cutting mat as a visual boundary. This simple solution cost less than $5 but proved invaluable in preventing accidental cross-contact during food preparation.

For those managing multiple dietary restrictions, maintaining separate utensils doesn't mean buying expensive sets. I found that wooden spoons and basic utensils from discount stores, marked with colored electrical tape on their handles, work just as effectively as pricier alternatives. The key is consistent use and proper labeling rather than the items' cost.

Budget-Friendly Utensil Management
- Colored electrical tape for marking handles

- Dedicated sponges for different zones

- Separate dish drying areas

- Basic utensil caddies for organization

- Washable cutting mats

My experience taught me that effective cleaning protocols don't require specialized products. A regular dish soap and hot water solution, followed by a vinegar-water spray, effectively cleans most surfaces. Mixing baking soda and water creates an abrasive, safe and economical paste for deeper cleaning.

Finding affordable solutions for shared appliances was one of the most challenging aspects of maintaining a safe kitchen. Instead of buying separate toasters and other small appliances, I invested in reusable toaster bags and appliance covers. These relatively inexpensive items allowed me to use shared equipment without the expense of purchasing duplicates safely.

The key to successful cross-contamination prevention lies in creating effective and sustainable systems. I developed a simple cleaning schedule using a basic whiteboard, ensuring that shared surfaces and equipment were adequately sanitized between uses. This systematic approach helped prevent costly mistakes while maintaining kitchen safety.

Budget-Friendly Cross-Contamination Prevention

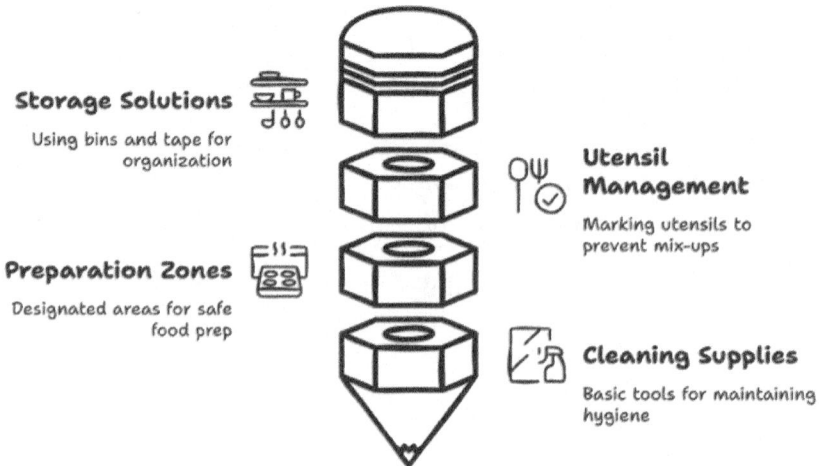

Storage Solutions
Using bins and tape for organization

Utensil Management
Marking utensils to prevent mix-ups

Preparation Zones
Designated areas for safe food prep

Cleaning Supplies
Basic tools for maintaining hygiene

Regarding meal prep, I discovered that batch cooking required careful planning to prevent cross-contamination. Rather than preparing everything simultaneously, I adopted a sequential approach: preparing allergen-free foods first, thoroughly cleaning work surfaces, and then handling other ingredients. This method required no additional equipment, just thoughtful organization of my cooking time.

Safe Meal Prep Essentials
- Basic timer for tracking cleaning intervals

- Disposable gloves from discount stores

- Washable prep station markers

- Budget-friendly cleaning supplies

- Simple storage labels

Remember that maintaining a safe kitchen environment doesn't require expensive equipment or specialty products. The essential elements are consistent practices, clear organization, and attention to detail. By focusing on these fundamentals, you can create a safe cooking space that protects against cross-contamination while respecting your budget constraints.

One beneficial strategy I developed was creating a 'clean as you go' station using a simple plastic tub filled with soapy water. This allowed me to immediately submerge used utensils and prevent accidental cross-contact during cooking sessions. The setup cost less than $10 but was invaluable in maintaining kitchen safety.

Clear communication and simple visual cues can prevent costly mistakes for those sharing kitchen space with others. I used inexpensive magnetic labels on my refrigerator and cabinets to indicate safe zones and potential allergen areas. This visual system helped roommates and family members maintain safety protocols without requiring constant reminders or expensive organizational tools.

The beauty of budget-friendly cross-contamination prevention lies in its simplicity. You can maintain a safe cooking environment without straining finances by focusing on basic principles and creative solutions. Remember, it's not about having the most expensive equipment – it's about developing consistent habits and innovative systems that protect your health while preserving your budget.

⚜

Batch Cooking for Restricted Diets: Maximizing Specialty Ingredients

Batch cooking with dietary restrictions requires a thoughtful approach to maximize specialty ingredients while minimizing costs. When I first started cooking gluten-free meals in batches, I quickly learned that success lies in scaling up recipes and strategically planning how to use expensive specialty ingredients across multiple dishes. This approach transformed my kitchen from a place of dietary challenges to a hub of efficient, budget-conscious meal preparation.

One of my most successful strategies has been the 'base component method.' Instead of preparing complete meals, I focus on cooking versatile ingredients that can be mixed and matched throughout the week. For example, when I find quinoa on sale, I'll cook a large batch plain, then portion it out to create different meals - from breakfast porridge with dairy-free milk to savory dinner bowls with roasted vegetables.

Base Components for Special Diets
- Plain cooked grains (quinoa, rice, millet)

- Roasted vegetable medleys

- Protein bases (beans, lentils, prepared meats)

- Homemade sauces and dressings

- Prepped fresh vegetables

The key to successful batch cooking with dietary restrictions is to focus on naturally compliant ingredients rather than expensive processed alternatives. When I prepare a large batch of roasted vegetables, I might use half for immediate meals and transform the other half into soup or grain bowl toppings. This approach not only saves money but also ensures variety in your meals.

I use a system I call the '3-2-1 method' for batch cooking with specialty ingredients. This involves preparing three protein options, two grain or starch bases, and one versatile sauce that complies with your dietary restrictions.

3 - 2- 1 Method

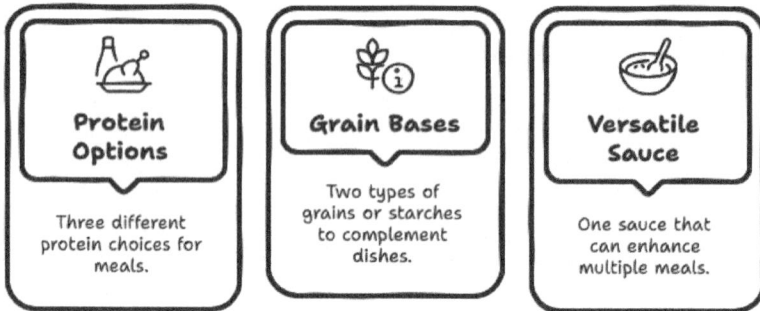

Protein Options	Grain Bases	Versatile Sauce
Three different protein choices for meals.	Two types of grains or starches to complement dishes.	One sauce that can enhance multiple meals.

This combination provides enough variety for a week's meals while controlling specialty ingredient costs.

Strategic Batch Cooking Tips

- Cook proteins in different seasonings for variety

- Prepare sauces that can be used in multiple ways

- Portion ingredients before combining

- Label everything with contents and date

- Plan complementary meals using similar ingredients

One of my most valuable lessons came from splurging on expensive almond flour for baking and deciding to make a large batch of gluten-free muffins. Unfortunately, I didn't properly store the remaining flour, which went rancid before I could use it again. Now, I portion specialty flours into freezer bags immediately after purchase, keeping only what I need for immediate use in the pantry.

When cooking with specialty ingredients in batches, proper storage becomes even more crucial due to the higher cost of these items. I invest in airtight containers and use my freezer strategically to extend the life of expensive ingredients. For example, I'll often make double batches of gluten-free flour blends when ingredients are on sale, storing the extra in the freezer for future use.

Storage Solutions for Specialty Ingredients
- Vacuum-sealed bags for flours and nuts

- Mason jars for prepared components

- Ice cube trays for portioned sauces

- Divided containers for prepped ingredients

- Freezer-safe bags for portioned meals

Meal variety is crucial when dealing with dietary restrictions to prevent food fatigue. Preparing versatile components allows for creative mixing and matching throughout the week. For instance, a batch of dairy-free cashew cream can become a pasta sauce one day, a soup base the next, and a vegetable dip later in the week.

Time management becomes critical when batch cooking with dietary restrictions. I organize my cooking sessions by temperature and equipment needs rather than by meal type. For example, while roasting vegetables in the oven, I'll simultaneously prepare a pot of quinoa on the stovetop and blend a batch of dairy-free sauce. This approach maximizes efficiency while minimizing the risk of cross-contamination.

Successful batch cooking with dietary restrictions isn't about making everything from scratch. Based on cost comparison and time investment, I strategically choose which components to prepare in bulk. Sometimes, finding a reliable commercial product for specific components allows me to focus my batch cooking efforts on items where I can significantly impact budget and quality.

Perhaps most importantly, I've learned to view dietary restrictions not as limitations but as creative challenges that push me to think more strategically about meal planning and preparation. Batch cooking can become a powerful tool for managing special dietary needs and budget constraints by focusing on versatile, naturally compliant ingredients and thoughtful preparation methods.

Multi-Diet Meal Planning: Accommodating Different Restrictions in One Kitchen

Managing multiple dietary restrictions in one kitchen is like conducting an orchestra where every instrument plays by different rules. When my sister moved in temporarily while dealing with celiac disease, and my partner decided to embrace a plant-based diet, our kitchen became a testing ground for accommodating diverse dietary needs without doubling our grocery budget or cooking time.

The key to successful multi-diet meal planning is finding common ground while maintaining individual dietary requirements. Rather than preparing completely separate meals, I use a modular meal system. This approach focuses on preparing versatile base ingredients customized to meet different nutritional needs, saving time and money while ensuring everyone's restrictions are respected.

Core Components for Multi-Diet Meals
- Protein options (plant-based and animal-based)

- Versatile grain bases (gluten-free and regular)

- Mixed vegetable preparations

- Adaptable sauces and seasonings

- Safe garnishes and toppings

Harmonizing Diverse Diets

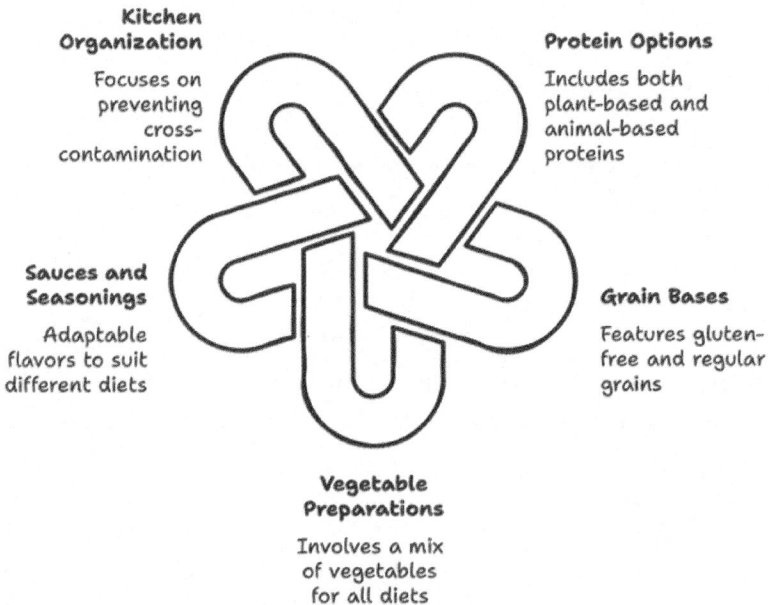

Kitchen Organization
Focuses on preventing cross-contamination

Protein Options
Includes both plant-based and animal-based proteins

Sauces and Seasonings
Adaptable flavors to suit different diets

Grain Bases
Features gluten-free and regular grains

Vegetable Preparations
Involves a mix of vegetables for all diets

One of my most successful strategies has been creating what I call 'compatibility zones' in the kitchen. We prevent cross-contamination while streamlining meal preparation by designating specific areas for different dietary needs and using a transparent color-coding system. The blue cutting board is exclusively for gluten-free preparation, while the green one is for plant-based ingredients.

Meal planning for multiple diets requires careful attention to ingredient overlap. I maintain a master list of ingredients that work for everyone, which becomes the foundation of our weekly menu. For example, roasted sweet potatoes, quinoa, and properly prepared legumes often serve as versatile bases that satisfy both gluten-free and plant-based requirements.

Shared Kitchen Organization
- Color-coded storage containers

- Designated preparation areas

- Separate cooking utensils

- Clear labeling systems

- Allergen-free zones

The 'build-your-own' meal concept has become a cornerstone of our multi-diet kitchen. Instead of trying to create single dishes that meet everyone's needs, I prepare various components that can be assembled according to individual dietary requirements. This approach accommodates different restrictions and empowers people to create meals that satisfy their preferences.

One particularly successful example of our modular approach is our weekly taco night. I prepare a base of seasoned black beans and roasted vegetables that everyone can eat, then offer various proteins, toppings, and wrapping options. Those following a gluten-free diet use corn tortillas, while others might choose whole wheat. Plant-based eaters consume extra vegetables and beans; others might add animal protein.

Flexible Meal Components
- Base vegetables and grains

- Multiple protein options

- Adaptable sauces and dressings

- Various wraps and bases

- Interchangeable toppings

Cost management becomes crucial when accommodating multiple diets. I focus on ingredients that naturally fit numerous dietary restrictions, reducing the need for expensive specialty products. For instance, many whole grains, legumes, and vegetables are naturally gluten-free and plant-based, making them excellent budget-friendly staples.

Meal prep timing is crucial when managing multiple diets. I typically start with the most restricted preparation (like gluten-free items) when surfaces and utensils are cleanest, then move on to other preparations. This systematic approach helps prevent cross-contamination while maintaining efficiency.

Perhaps most importantly, I've learned that successful multi-diet meal planning requires open communication and flexibility. We regularly discuss menu plans as a household, sharing ideas for adaptations and alternatives that can work for everyone. This collaborative approach makes meal planning more effective and helps everyone feel included and considered.

Remember that accommodating multiple diets doesn't mean cooking separate meals from scratch. Instead, focus on creating adaptable base recipes that can be modified to meet different dietary needs. This approach saves time, reduces costs, and makes meal preparation more manageable while ensuring everyone's nutritional requirements are met with delicious, satisfying options. As we conclude our exploration of managing special diets on a budget, it's clear that dietary restrictions don't have to mean financial strain or culinary compromise. Throughout this chapter, we've discovered that strategic planning, creative substitutions, and savvy shopping techniques can accommodate various dietary needs while maintaining a reasonable food budget.

By focusing on naturally compliant whole foods rather than expensive specialty products, learning to source ingredients from international markets, and mastering the art of homemade alternatives, I could transform my kitchen into a space that accommodated my dietary needs while keeping costs manageable.

The key lessons from this chapter extend beyond just managing costs. Using simple colour-coding systems and thoughtful kitchen organization, we've explored how to prevent cross-contamination without expensive specialty equipment. We've discovered the power of batch cooking with specialty ingredients, learning to maximize their use across multiple meals. And perhaps most importantly, we've seen how to accommodate various dietary restrictions in one kitchen through modular meal planning and strategic preparation techniques.

As you implement these strategies in your kitchen, remember that adapting to dietary restrictions is a journey, not a destination. Start with the basics - organizing your kitchen, identifying your go-to affordable alternatives, and building a repertoire of flexible recipes. Over time, you'll develop a system that meets your dietary needs and budget constraints.

The 'build-your-own' meal concept we discussed can become your secret weapon for accommodating multiple diets while maintaining budget control. By preparing versatile components that can be mixed and matched, you'll naturally create satisfying and cost-effective meals, regardless of dietary restrictions.

Moving forward, challenge yourself to view dietary restrictions not as limitations but as opportunities to explore new ingredients and cooking techniques. Each shopping trip becomes a chance to discover affordable alternatives, each cooking session an opportunity to perfect your cross-contamination prevention techniques, and each meal an occasion to celebrate the diversity of dietary needs while maintaining your budget goals.

Remember, successfully managing special diets on a budget comes from combining knowledge with practice. Start with the most manageable strategies for your situation, and gradually incorporate more techniques as you become comfortable. With time and patience, you'll find that maintaining a special diet can be both economically sustainable and culinarily satisfying.

Chapter Eight

Budget-Friendly Entertainment

Hosting Without the High Costs

The doorbell chimed as my first dinner party guests arrived, and I smiled, knowing that the entire evening's menu had cost less than a single restaurant entree. The art of budget-friendly entertaining has transformed my social life, proving that meaningful connections don't require expensive ingredients or elaborate decorations. Entertaining on a budget has become an art form in my kitchen, where creativity and careful planning always trump costly ingredients. The secret lies in understanding that memorable gatherings aren't about lavish spreads or costly decorations – they're about creating an atmosphere where connections flourish and conversations flow naturally.

Over the years, I've discovered that budget-friendly entertaining often leads to more meaningful experiences. When we strip away the pressure to impress with expensive ingredients or elaborate presentations, we create space for authentic connections and shared experiences. It's about mastering the delicate balance between being a welcoming host and a savvy budget manager.

My journey into budget-friendly entertainment began with what I now fondly call 'The $50 Dinner Party Challenge.' After lamenting how hosting had become too expensive, I tested whether I could create a memorable evening for six friends with just $50 for food and decorations. Using my meal planning skills, I transformed simple ingredients into an inviting Mediterranean-themed spread: homemade flatbreads, a hearty lentil soup, and a colorful seasonal salad. For the ambience, I created centrepieces using mason jars filled with fresh herbs from my garden and tea lights that I already owned. The evening was so successful that my friends didn't believe the total cost until I showed them my receipts. That night taught me that hospitality isn't about expensive ingredients or elaborate decorations – it's about creating a welcoming space for connection. This experience became the foundation for all my future entertaining, showing me that hosting can be both budget-friendly and beautiful with careful planning and creativity.

In this chapter, we'll explore practical strategies for hosting gatherings that won't strain your wallet. From potluck coordination to creative menu planning, you'll discover how to create inviting spaces and memorable experiences without excessive spending. We'll delve into techniques for transforming simple ingredients into impressive dishes, organizing group meals effectively, and maintaining the warmth of hospitality while adhering to a careful budget.

Whether planning a casual game night, a holiday celebration, or a simple dinner with friends, you'll learn how to navigate the entertaining world with confidence and financial wisdom. The key is to focus on what truly matters – bringing people together to share food, conversation, and connection in a welcoming environment that doesn't require breaking the bank.

Strategic Menu Planning: Crowd-Pleasing Dishes on a Budget

When planning menus for gatherings, the key is to focus on impressive and economical dishes. I learned this lesson while hosting monthly dinner clubs in my tiny apartment, where I discovered that some of the most beloved crowd-pleasers were also the most budget-friendly. The secret lies in choosing recipes that transform humble ingredients into memorable dishes through thoughtful preparation and creative presentation.

One of my go-to strategies is building menus around versatile base ingredients that can be dressed up in multiple ways. For instance, a large pot of perfectly cooked rice can become the foundation for a vibrant rice bowl station, where guests can customize their meals with an array of colorful toppings. I typically offer roasted seasonal vegetables, protein options like slow-cooked beans or shredded chicken, and a variety of homemade sauces. This approach stretches your budget and naturally accommodates different dietary preferences.

Budget-Friendly Entertaining Strategies

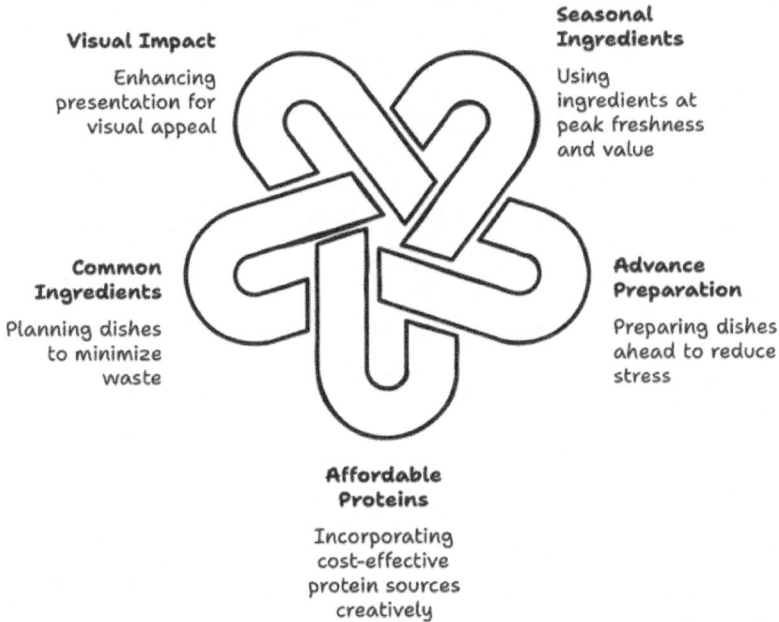

Visual Impact

Enhancing
presentation for
visual appeal

**Seasonal
Ingredients**

Using
ingredients at
peak freshness
and value

**Common
Ingredients**

Planning dishes
to minimize
waste

**Advance
Preparation**

Preparing dishes
ahead to reduce
stress

**Affordable
Proteins**

Incorporating
cost-effective
protein sources
creatively

Strategic menu planning also involves understanding how to create visual impact without expensive ingredients. Thoughtful plating and color combinations can elevate simple dishes into stunning presentations. A humble vegetable soup becomes a showstopper when garnished with fresh herbs and served in beautiful bowls. Even basic pasta dishes transform into elegant offerings when finished with a sprinkle of fresh herbs and a drizzle of good olive oil.

One of my most successful entertaining strategies is to create a centerpiece dish approach. Rather than preparing multiple elaborate dishes, I make one stunning main dish surrounded by simple, complementary sides. For example, a large, beautifully presented paella becomes the talk of the evening, while simple roasted vegetables and a fresh salad round out the meal without stretching the budget.

When planning quantities, I've developed a reliable formula that prevents shortages and excessive leftovers. I calculate about 6 ounces of protein per person for main dishes, adding 20% extra for varying appetites. For side dishes, I plan on ½ cup of each option per person, again adding a small buffer.

This approach ensures generous portions while maintaining budget control.

- Plan 1-2 show-stopping dishes rather than many elaborate options

- Calculate portions carefully to minimize waste

- Consider dishes that taste even better the next day

- Include make-ahead items to reduce day-of stress

- Balance hot and cold dishes for easier serving

The timing of your menu is just as important as the dishes themselves. I organize my menu planning around a detailed timeline, working backward from serving time to ensure everything comes together smoothly. This approach reduces stress and helps manage kitchen resources efficiently, which is particularly important when working with limited equipment or space.

Remember that successful budget-friendly entertaining often means embracing simplicity. Some of my most memorable gatherings have featured one-pot meals like hearty stews or baked pasta dishes that feed a crowd without straining resources. These dishes allow you to focus on quality ingredients that matter most while keeping the overall cost per person reasonable.

When planning your menu, consider creating a flexible feast. Dishes that can be easily adapted to accommodate different dietary needs without requiring separate preparations. For example, a build-your-own taco bar allows guests to customize their meals while you maintain budget control through strategic ingredient choices. This approach ensures everyone feels included while keeping costs manageable.

- Embrace one-pot meals that feed a crowd efficiently

- Create interactive dining experiences that stretch ingredients

- Plan dishes that work well at room temperature

- Include options that can be prepared days ahead

- Focus on crowd-pleasing classics with creative twists

The success of budget-friendly entertainment ultimately lies in thoughtful planning and creative presentation. By focusing on seasonal ingredients, thoughtful portion planning, and strategic recipe selection, you can create memorable gatherings that delight your guests without depleting your resources. Remember, it's not about how much you spend but how thoughtfully you plan and execute your menu.

Potluck Organization: Coordinating Shared Meals Successfully

Potlucks have become my secret weapon for hosting gatherings without straining my budget. What started as a simple solution to share hosting duties has evolved into an art form of coordinating delicious, varied meals where everyone contributes meaningfully. The key to a successful potluck organization lies in thoughtful planning and clear communication, ensuring a balanced meal while making participants feel confident about their contributions.

One of the most successful potluck strategies I utilize is a food color wheel. Instead of assigning specific dishes, I create a visual guide dividing contributions into color categories - greens, reds, yellows, and whites. This approach ensures a varied spread while giving participants creative freedom within their assigned color. For instance, someone assigned 'green' might bring a fresh salad, roasted Brussels sprouts, or herb-infused quinoa. This system prevents duplicate dishes and creates a visually stunning table encouraging healthy eating through natural variety.

- Create a shared digital signup sheet for tracking contributions

- Assign broad categories rather than specific dishes

- Consider dietary restrictions when planning categories

- Provide serving size guidelines based on guest count

- Suggest budget-friendly options within each category

Temperature and timing management is crucial for potluck success. I learned this lesson hard during an early hosting experience when we had twelve room-temperature dishes and no way to heat them simultaneously. Now, I create a balanced mix of hot and cold dishes, considering my available heating and cooling capacity. I provide contributors with specific arrival times staggered by dish type - cold dishes arrive first, followed by items needing heating, ensuring everything reaches the table at its proper temperature.

Successful Potluck Coordination Strategies

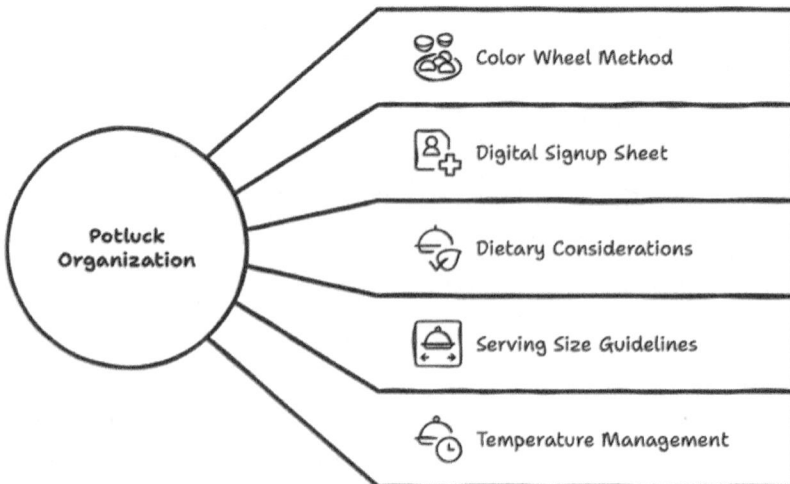

The logistics of serving ware can make or break a potluck gathering. I have created a 'Potluck Basics Box' - a collection of serving spoons, trivets, extension cords for slow cookers, and adhesive labels for identifying dishes and their ingredients. This preparation ensures smooth serving even when contributors forget serving utensils or need last-minute heating solutions.

- Coordinate serving temperatures and arrival times

- Plan electrical outlet needs for heating devices

- Provide clear labeling for allergens and ingredients

- Have extra serving utensils and containers available

- Create a designated space for each temperature category

Communication is the cornerstone of successful potluck coordination. I've developed a simple but effective system using a shared online spreadsheet that includes what people bring and key details like serving temperature, allergen information, and heating or cooling needs. This transparency helps everyone plan accordingly and ensures a well-balanced meal.

One of my favorite potluck innovations is a dedicated space where contributors can place recipe cards for their dishes. This helps with allergen awareness and builds community as participants share their culinary knowledge. I provide simple template cards with spaces for ingredients, instructions, and estimated cost per serving, making it easy for others to recreate budget-friendly favorites at home.

I've developed a reliable formula for portion planning that helps contributors determine appropriate quantities.

How to effectively plan food portions for a gathering?

Main Dishes

Aim for 4-6 ounces per person to provide a satisfying meal

Side Dishes

Plan for ½ cup per person to complement the meal

I always recommend that contributors multiply their planned portions by 1.5 to ensure enough food without creating excessive leftovers.

- Share clear portion guidelines with contributors

- Plan for dietary restrictions and preferences

- Organize a system for leftover distribution

- Consider storage needs for different types of dishes

- Provide guidance on transportation methods

The success of a potluck often depends on how well you manage the flow of the meal. I arrange dishes logically, starting with appetizers and moving through to desserts, with clear signage indicating each section. This organization helps prevent bottlenecks and ensures everyone can easily find and enjoy all contributions.

Remember that the goal of a potluck isn't just to share the cost of hosting - it's about creating a collaborative dining experience where everyone contributes to the meal's success. You can coordinate budget-friendly and deliciously memorable potlucks by providing clear guidelines while maintaining flexibility.

DIY Decor and Atmosphere: Creating Ambiance Without High Costs

Creating an inviting atmosphere for entertaining doesn't require expensive decorations or elaborate setups. I discovered this truth on a tight budget during my first holiday season when I transformed my modest apartment into a warm, welcoming space using items I already owned and natural elements from my garden. The secret lies in understanding that ambience comes from thoughtful details and creative arrangements rather than costly decorative pieces.

One of my most successful entertaining transformations began with the theme of the 'Light and Nature' approach. Instead of purchasing expensive decorations, I focused on creating layers of soft lighting using existing lamps, candles, and string lights I already owned. Combining these with natural elements like fresh herbs, seasonal branches, and citrus fruits created an enchanting atmosphere that engaged multiple senses without straining my budget.

Budget-Friendly Ambiance Creation

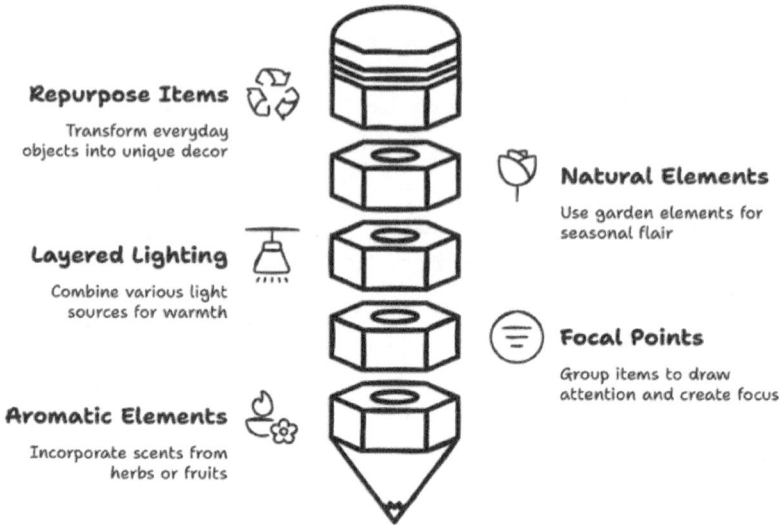

Repurpose Items
Transform everyday
objects into unique decor

Natural Elements
Use garden elements for
seasonal flair

Layered Lighting
Combine various light
sources for warmth

Focal Points
Group items to draw
attention and create focus

Aromatic Elements
Incorporate scents from
herbs or fruits

The art of budget-friendly decorating often involves seeing the potential in ordinary items. Mason jars become elegant candle holders, brown paper bags transform into luminaries, and simple white dishes grouped create striking displays. The key is to focus on composition rather than individual pieces - grouping similar items together often creates more visual impact than scattered expensive decorations.

One of my favorite money-saving decoration techniques is to scavenge seasonally. Each season offers its free decorative bounty - fallen leaves in autumn, pine cones in winter, wildflowers in spring, and garden herbs in summer. I create centrepieces that rival expensive floral arrangements by combining these natural elements with simple glass containers or baskets I own.

The power of lighting cannot be overstated when creating an atmosphere. I've developed a three-layer lighting approach that transforms any space: ambient lighting for overall illumination, task lighting for functional areas, and accent lighting for the atmosphere. Using a combination of existing lamps, tea lights in mason jars, and strategically placing mirrors to reflect light, I create a warm, inviting glow without purchasing specialty lighting fixtures.

- Position mirrors to maximize natural and artificial light

- Use white linens to brighten spaces naturally

- Create height variation in decorative groupings

- Incorporate metallic elements for light reflection

- Use fabric remnants for table runners and accents

Music is crucial in setting the mood but doesn't require an expensive sound system. I create carefully curated playlists that match the gathering's energy, using my existing devices and speakers positioned strategically around the space. The key is selecting music that enhances conversation rather than overwhelming it.

One of my most successful entertaining innovations is to use static decorations; I create areas where guests can participate in the ambience. For example, a simple glass bowl filled with water and floating candles becomes more engaging when guests are invited to add flower petals or herbs throughout the evening. This not only saves money on elaborate centerpieces but also creates memorable experiences.

Temperature and scent contribute significantly to the atmosphere. Rather than purchasing expensive candles or air fresheners, I simmer natural ingredients like citrus peels, cinnamon sticks, and fresh herbs on the stovetop. This creates a welcoming aroma and adds humidity to the air during dry seasons. The bonus is that many of these ingredients can be used in cooking afterwards, preventing waste.

- Simmer natural aromatics for ambient scent

- Use fabric scraps for napkin rings and decorative touches

- Create themed vignettes with existing items

- Incorporate seasonal produce as decor elements

- Repurpose glass containers for candle holders

The art of table setting can transform a simple meal into an elegant experience without additional cost. I mix and match existing dishes, creating interest through thoughtful arrangement rather than matching sets. Simple white dishes become sophisticated when combined with natural elements and careful placement. Even mismatched glasses can become a charming feature when arranged intentionally.

Remember that the most memorable gatherings often have more to do with the warmth of the atmosphere than the cost of the decorations. You can create inviting spaces that welcome guests without straining your budget by focusing on creative arrangement, natural elements, and thoughtful lighting. The key is to see the potential in what you already have and let your creativity guide the transformation.

※

Entertainment Ideas: Budget-Friendly Activities and Games

Entertainment doesn't have to drain your wallet when hosting gatherings. Through years of hosting on a budget, I've discovered that some of the most memorable evenings center around simple, engaging activities that cost little to nothing. The key is focusing on interactions and shared experiences rather than expensive entertainment options.

Another successful discovery is a cooking-related challenge that requires only essential pantry items. For instance, the mystery ingredient challenge involves participants creating simple appetizers using surprise ingredients from my pantry. This provides entertainment and often results in discovering creative new recipes that become part of our regular rotation.

Music-based entertainment can transform an evening without any additional cost. Musical Memory Lane is an interactive idea where each guest shares a significant song and the story behind it. This creates a natural conversation flow and personal connections without additional resources beyond existing devices or speakers.

Outdoor spaces offer endless possibilities for free entertainment. I've organized everything from stargazing sessions with homemade constellation maps to nature scavenger hunts using items found in local parks. These activities cost nothing and create unique experiences that wouldn't be possible in traditional entertainment venues.

- Organize nature walks with educational components

- Create photo challenges using smartphone cameras

- Plan collaborative art projects with household supplies

- Arrange skill-sharing sessions among guests

- Design simple scavenger hunts around your home

Interactive food activities provide both entertainment and sustenance. My 'Build-Your-Own' stations - for tacos, pizzas, or desserts - turn meal preparation into a social activity. Guests enjoy the creative process while naturally engaging in conversation and collaboration.

For more structured entertainment, I've developed a collection of printable game templates that can be reused multiple times. Simple word games, drawing challenges, and trivia questions printed on cardstock become durable entertainment options that cost only the initial printing fee. These games often spark more engagement than expensive board games because they suit your group's interests.

One particularly successful activity I have created has the guests each take turns teaching a simple skill - from folding origami to basic juggling. This provides entertainment, creates valuable learning experiences, and strengthens community bonds.

- Develop reusable game templates for various occasions

- Create themed charade cards using recycled materials

- Design collaborative storytelling prompts

- Organize simple talent showcases

- Plan group singing or music-making sessions

The key to successful budget-friendly entertainment is understanding that people crave interaction more than elaborate activities. Simple games that encourage conversation and creativity often create more memorable experiences than expensive entertainment. The most successful gatherings focus on activities that allow everyone to participate while feeling comfortable and engaged.

Remember that timing and pacing are crucial when planning activities. I typically plan for 2-3 different activity options per gathering, allowing natural transitions between them based on the group's energy and interests. This flexibility ensures that the entertainment remains engaging without feeling forced or overwhelming.

The beauty of budget-friendly entertainment is that it often creates more authentic connections than costly alternatives. By focusing on interactive experiences and creative engagement, you can host memorable gatherings that unite people without straining your resources. The key is to remember that the best entertainment facilitates connections rather than simply filling time.

꙳ᠵᠵᠵᠵ ᠊᠊᠊᠊꙳

Seasonal Celebration Strategies: Holiday Hosting Without Overspending

Holiday celebrations often bring the most significant challenges to budget-conscious hosts. I learned this lesson during my first year of budget entertaining when I attempted to recreate my mother's elaborate Christmas dinner on a fraction of the budget. What began as a stressful endeavor evolved into a valuable lesson in prioritizing meaningful traditions while managing costs. The secret, I discovered, lies in thoughtful planning and creative adaptations of holiday classics.

Budget-Friendly Holiday Hosting

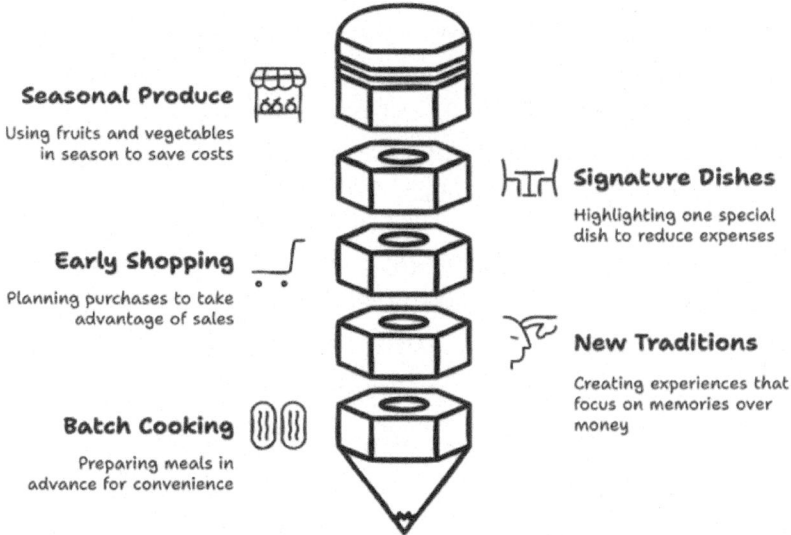

Seasonal Produce
Using fruits and vegetables in season to save costs

Signature Dishes
Highlighting one special dish to reduce expenses

Early Shopping
Planning purchases to take advantage of sales

New Traditions
Creating experiences that focus on memories over money

Batch Cooking
Preparing meals in advance for convenience

One of my most successful approaches to hosting holiday entertaining is instead of including every traditional dish, I focus on one or two signature items that carry a special meaning and then complement them with budget-friendly sides. For instance, I might splurge on a small, high-quality ham but surround it with cost-effective, seasonal vegetable dishes and homemade bread.

- Plan menus around seasonal produce at peak availability

- Focus on one special dish rather than multiple expensive items

- Start shopping early to take advantage of sales

- Create new traditions that emphasize experience over expense

- Utilize batch cooking for make-ahead dishes

Decorating for holiday gatherings doesn't require expensive seasonal items. I've developed a collection of versatile decorative elements that can be styled differently for each holiday. Simple white tablecloths become festive with natural additions like pine branches in winter or autumn leaves in fall. Mason jars filled with battery-operated lights create magical centerpieces that can be used year-round.

Timing is crucial for holiday hosting success. I maintain a detailed calendar marking when seasonal items are on sale and plan my shopping accordingly. This strategy allows me to gradually stock up on non-perishable items and frozen goods when prices are lowest rather than paying premium prices closer to the holiday.

One of the most effective cost-saving techniques I utilize is to combine a few signature dishes with a coordinated potluck element instead of providing all the food myself. I provide the main dish and one or two special items, then guide guests on bringing complementary dishes that fit the theme and their budget.

- Create a detailed shopping timeline to catch sales

- Use versatile decorations that work for multiple holidays

- Implement a hybrid hosting model combining provided and potluck dishes

- Focus on make-ahead dishes to reduce day-of stress

- Plan for strategic leftover usage

Leftover management becomes crucial during holiday hosting. I plan my menu with intentional leftovers in mind, ensuring that excess food can be repurposed into new meals or frozen for future use. For example, leftover turkey becomes the base for soup, sandwiches, and casseroles, while extra vegetables transform into creative side dishes or additions to breakfast scrambles.

Drinks can quickly inflate a holiday gathering's budget. Instead of providing a full bar, I create one unique holiday beverage - perhaps a festive punch or mulled wine - and complement it with water infused with seasonal fruits and herbs. This approach feels special while keeping costs manageable.

The pressure to provide elaborate gifts or party favors can strain holiday budgets. Simple, homemade touches often create more meaningful memories than expensive purchases. Sending guests home with small portions of a special dish or providing recipe cards for favorite holiday treats creates lasting connections without significant expense.

- Create one signature holiday beverage instead of a full bar

- Plan intentional leftovers for future meals

- Make homemade party favors using kitchen staples

- Focus on creating memories through shared experiences

- Maintain a holiday budget tracking system

Perhaps the most valuable lesson I've learned about holiday hosting is that guests remember the warmth and welcome of a gathering far more than its elaborate details. By focusing on creating a welcoming atmosphere and meaningful connections, you can host memorable holiday celebrations that honor traditions without overwhelming your budget.

Successful holiday hosting on a budget requires advanced planning and thoughtful prioritization. By focusing on what matters most to you and your guests, you can create memorable and abundant celebrations while maintaining financial wisdom. The key is to remember that the heart of any holiday gathering lies in the connections we make, not the amount we spend. Reflecting on the transformative power of budget-friendly entertaining, I'm reminded of that pivotal $50 dinner party that changed my approach to hosting. The journey from seeing entertaining as a financial burden to discovering it as an opportunity for creative connection has been enlightening and empowering. Through careful planning, thoughtful menu design, and innovative approaches to ambience, I've learned that memorable gatherings don't require extravagant spending.

The strategies we've explored in this chapter - from strategic menu planning to DIY decor solutions - demonstrate that hosting on a budget is not about limitation but rather a creative possibility. We've seen how potluck coordination can transform group meals into collaborative celebrations and how simple entertainment ideas can spark genuine connection without straining resources. The seasonal celebration strategies we've discussed prove that even holiday hosting can be both festive and financially responsible.

Perhaps most importantly, we've discovered that the true essence of entertaining lies not in elaborate spreads or expensive decorations but in creating spaces where genuine connections can flourish. We can host abundant and special gatherings while maintaining financial wisdom by focusing on thoughtful planning, creative use of resources, and intentional atmosphere creation.

As you progress with your entertaining journey, remember that every budget constraint invites innovation. Whether planning an intimate dinner party or a holiday celebration, the principles we've explored - from strategic shopping to creative repurposing - will help you create memorable and financially responsible gatherings.

The art of budget-friendly entertaining ultimately teaches us that hospitality is about opening our homes and hearts, not our wallets. By embracing this mindset and applying the practical strategies we've discussed, you can create warm, welcoming gatherings that unite people without breaking the bank. After all, the most treasured memories from any gathering rarely center on how much was spent but rather on the connections formed and shared joy.

Let's start small as we close this chapter, perhaps with your version of the $50 dinner party challenge. Let each gathering be an opportunity to refine your approach to budget-conscious hosting, always remembering that the most meaningful celebrations are built on thoughtful planning, creative solutions, and genuine hospitality rather than excessive spending. With these tools and strategies, you're well-equipped to host economical and unforgettable gatherings.

Conclusion

As we conclude our journey together, I am reminded of a pivotal moment in my kitchen during the 2008 recession when necessity sparked a transformation in my approach to cooking and meal planning. What began as a desperate attempt to reduce expenses has blossomed into a fulfilling lifestyle that demonstrates eating well and spending wisely aren't mutually exclusive.

Throughout this book, we have explored the fundamental building blocks of budget-conscious cooking, from mastering innovative shopping strategies to transforming leftovers into exciting new meals. We have discovered that a well-organized kitchen is not just about aesthetics; it serves as the foundation for sustainable savings and efficient meal preparation. The techniques we've covered, from batch cooking in small spaces to scaling recipes for different household sizes, prove that anyone can create delicious, nutritious meals while adhering to a careful budget with the right approach.

I have shared my struggles and victories, which have taught me the importance of proper storage and that hospitality does not require extravagance. These experiences, along with the practical strategies and tips throughout this book, show that budget meal planning is more than just a collection of money-saving techniques; it is a pathway to greater food security, reduced waste, and more confident cooking.

The skills you've gained—ranging from navigating different store types to adapting recipes for dietary restrictions—are tools that will benefit you beyond the kitchen. They signify a fundamental shift in the way we think about food, cooking, and resource management. Whether you are cooking for one or feeding a family, these principles will help you create satisfying meals while fostering a more sustainable and economical approach to food.

As you continue your journey, remember that every small change can lead to significant savings. Start with one strategy that resonates with you, whether it's implementing a weekly meal prep routine or mastering the art of creative leftover transformation. Build your confidence gradually, and don't hesitate to adapt these techniques to fit your unique circumstances.

Looking back at my transformation from someone who relied heavily on takeout to becoming an efficient, budget-conscious cook, I am struck by how this journey has enriched my life beyond mere financial savings. It has fostered creativity, reduced stress, and created opportunities for meaningful connections through shared meals. I hope this book serves as more than just a guide to saving money; may it be your companion in discovering the joy and satisfaction of mindful, budget-friendly cooking.

Successful budget meal planning is not about deprivation or bland, repetitive meals. It is about making informed choices, being creative with resources, and enjoying the process of preparing nourishing food. As you apply these principles in your kitchen, you may discover—just as I did—that some of the most satisfying meals arise not from expensive ingredients but from thoughtful preparation and creative problem-solving.

The skills and strategies shared in these pages provide the foundation for a more economical and sustainable approach to cooking. Use them as building blocks, adapting and expanding upon them as you develop your own style of budget-conscious cooking. Your journey toward more mindful, cost-effective meal planning is just beginning, and I am confident that with these tools at your disposal, you will create your own success story in the kitchen.

May your pantry be well-stocked, your meals be satisfying, and your budget remain healthy as you explore the rewarding world of budget-conscious cooking. Here's to saving money while eating better, one thoughtfully planned meal at a time.

Julie x

Also By

Julie Anne Summers

Growing Up at The Table : Your Child'd Journey Through Food

Balanced Plate: A Comprehensive Guide to Pre-Diabetes Nutrition and Meal Prep

Fit and Fifty : A Joint Journey to Health and Wellness

Balanced Table : Finding Joy and Freedom in Mindful Eating

A Life Renewed : Overcoming Challenges and Celebrating Success in Later Years

About the Author

Julie Anne Summers

With over a decade of experience transforming a bustling takeout kitchen into a thriving meal prep sanctuary, the author has perfected the art of budget-friendly cooking while balancing a demanding career.

Having mastered the challenge of feeding a household on a tight budget, they are passionate about empowering others to discover the joy of efficient, cost-effective meal planning that doesn't compromise on flavor or nutrition.

An avid gardener, the author is currently cultivating their dream garden, embracing a healthy lifestyle and deepening their connection with nature. In a world where health and nutrition form the bedrock of a fulfilling life, they fervently believe in the importance of seeking medical support when necessary, and in maintaining an active lifestyle for longevity and vitality.

With a diverse background spanning natural resources, paramedicine, and human resources, the author is driven by a mission to make a positive impact and leave the world better than they found it.

Through their heartfelt writing, they invite readers to explore insights and experiences that inspire a commitment to healthy living and a profound connection with the natural world, guiding them on a journey toward an active and vibrant life.

References / Bibliography

- American Academy of Pediatrics. (2019).Pediatric Nutrition Handbook, 8th Edition. Elk Grove Village, IL: AmericanAcademy of Pediatrics.

- Brown, J.E. (2019). Nutrition Through theLife Cycle, 7th Edition. Boston, MA: Cengage Learning.

- AnthonyPorto, M.D., and Dina DiMaggio, M.D. (2016) The Pediatrician's Guide to FeedingBabies and Toddlers: Practical Answers to Your Questions on Nutrition, StartingSolids, Allergies, Picky Eating, and More. Clarkson Potter/Ten Speed Press

- Satter,E. (1986). Child of Mine: Feeding with Love and Good Sense. Boulder, CO: BullPublishing Company. (Third Edition 2012)

- Rapley, G. & Murkett, T. (2019). Baby-LedWeaning: The Essential Guide. New York: The Experiment Publishing.

- Satter,E. (2008). Secrets of Feeding a Healthy Family. Madison, WI: Kelcy Press.

- Thompson,J. & Manore, M. (2018). Nutrition: An Applied Approach, 5th Edition. NewYork: Pearson.

- USDA & U.S. Department of Health andHuman Services. (2020). Dietary Guidelines for Americans, 2020-2025, 9thEdition. Washington, DC: U.S. Government Printing Office.

Printed in Dunstable, United Kingdom